1993

IDENTIFYING
IVAN

IDENTIFYING IVAN

A CASE STUDY IN LEGAL PSYCHOLOGY

WILLEM A. WAGENAAR

Harvard University Press
Cambridge, Massachusetts
1988

10 9 8 7 6 5 4 3 2 1

Library of Congress Cataloging-in-Publication Data

Wagenaar, Willem Albert, 1941–
    Identifying Ivan: a case study in legal psychology/Willem A.
Wagenaar.
        p.   cm.
    Bibliography: p.
    ISBN 0–874–44285–7
    1. Demjanjuk, John—Trials, litigation, etc.   2. War crime trials—
Jerusalem.   3. Evidence. Criminal   4. Psychology, Forensic.
5. Crime and criminals—Identification.   I. Title.
JX5441.D45W35 1989
341.6'9'02685694—dc19   88–27571
                                                                    CIP

Contents

List of Tables

List of Figures

Preface

In the period 1987–88 John Demjanjuk was tried before a special court in Jerusalem. The charge was that, as 'Ivan the Terrible', he had killed 850,000 people in the gas chambers of Treblinka. I acted as a defense witness, testifying about problems of identification by eyewitnesses. This book is a reflection upon my testimony and the scientific knowledge on which it rested. Therefore, it is more a case study in legal psychology than a textbook. The topics were selected for discussion on the basis of their relevance for the case of Ivan. But I believe that the same, or very similar, issues are at stake in many other cases in which experimental psychologists act as expert witnesses.

The major reason for writing a case study on the identification of Ivan, and not on one of the many other cases in which I have been involved, is that Ivan's case is better suited for a demonstration of the many problems of identification by eyewitnesses than any in my experience. I know of no other case in which so many deviations from procedures internationally accepted as desirable occurred.

The second reason for making the case of Ivan my example is that it provides a very good illustration of the role of expert testimony. The legal proof of Demjanjuk's identity was based on identification evidence exclusively. The courts in Cleveland and Jerusalem accepted this evidence in every respect. The Cleveland court refused to hear an expert witness on identification problems. The Jerusalem court allowed the defense to bring forward an expert, but declared that the testimony was irrelevant because the surviving witnesses could not make mistakes. This reaction is not atypical and provides a useful lesson to defense counsel and expert witnesses alike. The logic of science is not judicially imperative, and expert testimony is weighed against other considerations of a totally different nature. The *a priori* beliefs of the members of a court are among these other considerations. The case of Ivan affords a revealing insight into what a court may reject as irrelevant.

The third reason for writing this book is that so many people have expressed interest in this case, although they appear to have a wrong conception of the facts and the contents of my testimony. Many people seem to believe that I testified that the memories of death camp survivors are not to be trusted after 40 years, and they rightly questioned whether science would allow such an assertion. Newspapers and other news media also found it extremely difficult to believe that I did not challenge the memories of death camp survivors. In this book I will try to explain that one cannot assess the reliability of the witnesses in this case because of the lack of scientific ground for making such assessments.

I may be accused of using the Ivan trial, with its strong association with the death of so many people in Treblinka, for the advancement of my own interests, and of riding on the wave of publicity given to this case. I hope that the readers of this book will appreciate my real motives.

The content of my testimony was limited to an analysis of the procedures used for the identification of John Demjanjuk as Ivan the Terrible. The reader may conclude that the procedures used for testing the memories of witnesses did not conform to the best legal and scientific standards, and that, therefore, the reliability of the eyewitnesses should be scrutinized carefully by the court. The court looked into this matter carefully, and decided to put full trust in the identifications, despite my testimony. After having read the material presented in this book, the reader might wonder about the court's decision. But apart from the enormity of the charge and the complexity of the material, the case is not exceptional. The investigations and the examination of eyewitnesses were no worse than in many other cases. Police investigations do not always match the standards of scientific research. Whether or not the investigations in a specific case meet the standards, has to be decided by the court, not by expert witnesses.

In Chapter 3, I propose rules that may help to improve the quality of identification procedures. These rules are an amalgam of principles that reflect the thinking of scholars and researchers, some of which has been enacted into law. But many of these guidelines, although widely recognized, have not been accepted wholly by any judicial body. I would feel that I have achieved an important objective if these rules were to be incorporated within standard investigative and legal practice throughout the world.

Another issue that will be omitted from my discussion is a considerable amount of evidence that has become available since my testimony in November 1987. Among this material there are statements by 15 witnesses who saw Ivan for varying periods, and who failed to identify John Demjanjuk, or who positively indicated that he was not Ivan, or who identified him as another person. Although the attempts at identification were made long ago, this material, the existence of which was known to the US prosecution throughout, only became available to the Israeli defense in 1988. Hence it was not available for use in my testimony.

Since this book is not a pamphlet for the defense of John Demjanjuk, I will not comment on the verdict of the Jerusalem court, which found him guilty and sentenced him to death. On the contrary, I would argue that an expert should not comment upon a court's verdict, because verdicts are outside the expert's domain. A verdict is never determined by expert testimony only. The combination of all relevant facts which form a final judgment is a complex task that goes far beyond the professional insights of an expert witness. In concrete terms this means that my discussion of the case will be limited to the material covered in my own testimony. The court's comments on this testimony and the reasons for the court's trust in the eyewitnesses' identifications that were presented in the Jerusalem trial should not, and will not, be discussed by me.

All material on the case of Ivan is drawn from official documents, such as the legal statements on identification attempts, and the transcripts of actual court sessions. These documents were translated into English by certified interpreters. Hence the English texts have an official status, and I did not venture to improve upon the English, even in those cases in which it was difficult to comprehend.

In the preparation of my testimony I was assisted by intense discussions with Professor Elizabeth Loftus of the University of Washington, and Professors James Reason and Sebastian Halliday, both from the University of Manchester. The manuscript profited from the many helpful comments given by Professor Maya Bar-Hillel from the Hebrew University, Professor Elizabeth Loftus of the University of Washington, and lawyer Yoram Sheftel. The English usage and style were improved by Kate Hudson. The preparation of various stages of the manuscript was in the hands of my invaluable colleagues Li Lian Brak and Ans Joustra.

Leiden, June 1988

1 Introduction

In 1976 John Demjanjuk, a factory worker from Cleveland, Ohio, was identified for the first time as Ivan the Terrible, the man who operated the gas chambers in the Nazi death camp near Treblinka, in Poland. Treblinka was an extermination camp in which the Germans killed over 850,000 Jews. The victims were transported by train to Treblinka from all over Europe. There they were unloaded and gassed on the day of their arrival. The unloading and preparation occurred in a part of the camp that was called Camp 1. The gas chambers and the ovens were located in Camp 2, which was shielded from Camp 1 by extensive camouflage. Ivan the Terrible used to work in Camp 2, where he distinguished himself by his cruelty to the victims, even in the few minutes before their deaths. The very idea that this horrible creature could still be alive, passing as an innocent family man, caused a shock around the world, and led to a number of legal actions against Demjanjuk in the United States and in Israel. In Cleveland, Ohio, Demjanjuk was first tried on the charge that he lied when he applied for American citizenship. This led to a revocation of his citizenship in 1981. In 1983 he was tried again before a Cleveland court, but now to have him extradited to Israel.

In Jerusalem in 1987–88 he was tried for Nazi crimes, which included the killing of those 850,000 Jews at Treblinka.

The remarkable aspect of this case is that John Demjanjuk denied from the very beginning that he was Ivan the Terrible, or that he had worked in any of the German

1

death camps. Hence the legal procedure was, to a large extent, dependent upon the proof of his identity. The prosecutors provided three types of evidence of his identity. 1. A number of survivors from Treblinka recognized him from a picture taken in 1951. 2. An identity card, made available by the government of the Soviet Union, revealed that an Ukrainian by the name of Ivan Demjanjuk was trained in the German camp Trawniki for service in concentration camps and death camps. 3. Demjanjuk's alibi was sparse and inconsistent and lacked a detailed account of his whereabouts between August 1942 and August 1943, the period in which Ivan was active in Treblinka. This book deals with the first item: the identification by surviving witnesses. The two other issues will be largely disregarded, with the exception of the picture on the Trawniki identity card, which was also used for identification. Thus the questions of whether the Trawniki card was genuine, whether there was an Ivan Demjanjuk in Treblinka, and whether this person was indeed Ivan the Terrible, will be left untouched. Nor will I discuss the question of whether the incomplete or inconsistent alibi proves that John Demjanjuk was deliberately lying about his past. Identification by surviving witnesses after 35 years is our theme. Nothing else.

THE EYEWITNESSES

The death camp Treblinka was situated in Poland, some 50 miles north-east of Warsaw. The gas chambers were constructed and came into operation during 1942. A more complete description of the camp is provided by Gitta Sereny in her book *Into that Darkness*, which is largely based upon interviews with Treblinka's commander, Franz Stangl. The camp was run by some 30–40 German guards, and over one hundred Ukrainian ex-prisoners of war, trained for special duties in Trawniki. But much of the real work, such as the sorting of clothes, the shaving of the female victims' hair, the removal of corpses from the gas chambers, the extraction of gold teeth from the bodies, the burial, and later, on Himmler's orders, the excavation and burning of corpses, was done by Jewish forced labor. These people were left alive as long as they could do their jobs, and as long as they escaped the arbitrary whims of their tormentors. They were employed in Camp 1, the area where the victims were received and prepared for their death, and in Camp 2, the location of the gas chambers. Ivan the Terrible, who was one of the operators of the diesel engine which produced the gas for the gas chambers, was for most of the time in Camp 2. Unlike other camps, such as Auschwitz and Dachau, Treblinka did not employ the victims for other forced labor before they were killed. Every victim entering Camp 2 was killed in due course. The only exceptions were a few work Jews, who escaped their fate in a miraculous manner.

In the late spring and early summer of 1943 the Jewish forced labor noticed that the transports of victims were becoming less and less frequent. This could only mean that there were no victims left, and that the camp would soon be closed, which implied the inescapable death of the remaining Jews. It was decided to attempt an uprising against the German and Ukrainian guards. Desperate as such an enterprise must have seemed, it was the only hope of escape. The uprising took place on August 2, 1943. Due to an unfortunate misunderstanding the prisoners in Camp 2 started too early. They began successfully, but soon were overrun by alerted troops from Camp 1, and from another nearby camp. A few people escaped to the nearby woods, and from there to various hiding places throughout Europe. Shortly after the uprising Treblinka was closed down, and those who did not escape were killed. All surviving witnesses who attempted the later identification of John Demjanjuk belonged to the group that escaped during the uprising.

THE IDENTIFICATION PROBLEM

A consequence of Treblinka's history is that there were few survivors, maybe 50 in all. But these survivors had more than a casual acquaintance with their German and Ukrainian guards. For a year or more they had the opportunity to watch them daily, and at close quarters. This included Ivan. Therefore it is highly surprising that the later identification by at least eight witnesses could still be questionable. But there were a number of problems. One was that, although some of the survivors worked close to Ivan, they never had any real contact with him. They never talked to him, or engaged in any joint activity. Indeed they avoided eye contact with him, and tried to stay out of his way, because any encounter with him could result in death. Thus nobody knew his real name. The name Demjanjuk was made public by the Soviets only in 1976. The first name, Ivan, could well have been a nickname. In fact the United Nations search list of war criminals mentions an Alfred Bielich, also known as Ivan the Terrible. Two survivors, Rosenberg and Rajchman, published short memoirs about their time in Treblinka soon after the war. Although Ivan the Terrible was one of the worst characters in the camp, few lines were spent on his description. Rosenberg did mention him but provided no description, Rajchman described him as 'a healthy, powerful horse', aged about 25. Thus, from the original testimonies we do not know Ivan's real name, his exact age, or how he looked. It was said that he was an Ukrainian.

Another problem was that there was no picture of John Demjanjuk to show how he looked in 1942–43. Demjanjuk was 22 in 1942. The picture used for identification was taken in 1951, when he emigrated to the United States. This picture (Fig. 1.d) shows him at the age of 31. A man can change substantially between the ages of 22 and 31. The picture on the Trawniki identity card (Fig. 1.b) was allegedly taken in 1942, but the authenticity of this picture is in dispute. Even should this picture represent John Demjanjuk at the age of 22 we have a problem: the Trawniki picture was shown to the witnesses after they had seen the 1951 portrait. Knowing how a person looks at the age of 30, it is less difficult to identify the same person from a parade containing a picture of that person at the age of 20. Another picture of Demjanjuk at the age of 28 or 29 (Fig 1.c) was discovered in 1987, after all the witnesses had already given testimony. A picture representing John Demjanjuk in a Red

Army uniform (Fig. 1.a) reveals little of his face and was not used for identification.

A third problem was that 35 years is a very long time. Too long for an identification parade to be held with John Demjanjuk as one of the actual participants. And it may be also too long for the survivors to be absolutely certain. This is a question we will discuss in detail later. For the moment it is sufficient to allude to the cases of Walus and Fedorenko, both accused of committing war crimes, both recognized by surviving witnesses who had seen them many times. In both cases the courts decided that the identification by eyewitnesses left too much room for doubt.

The question of whether survivors of Nazi death camps can completely forget the faces of their tormentors raises many emotions. But the question is wrong. The issue is not that Ivan's face is completely or substantially forgotten, but that a slight fading of the memory over 35 years has occurred, just enough to render possible confusion with another person, who looks very similar. Even when it is assumed that survivors of death camps have accurate memories, it is still customary to accept such memories as proof in a capital case only after substantial testing. The normal form of such a test is the identity parade, and Ivan's prosecutors did not challenge this principle.

THE QUESTIONABLE LOGIC OF IDENTITY PARADES

After 35 years it was not possible to include John Demjanjuk in a live parade. Therefore it was decided to compose an identity parade of photos, including the 1951 picture of Demjanjuk. The logic of such a photo identity parade is simple. A picture of the suspect is arranged within a larger set of similar pictures, representing innocent others, the so-called foils. Witnesses without an accurate memory of the face of the perpetrator are expected to state that they do not recognize anyone. If they fail to make such a cautious response, they are expected to pick one of the pictures on an arbitrary basis, which means that there is no greater

Figure 1.1: Four photographs of John Demjanjuk.

preference for the target picture than for any of the foils. Only those eyewitnesses who remember the face accurately will be able to select the target picture without hesitation, provided that the suspect is the same person as the perpetrator. The situation can be represented as in Table 1.1.

Table 1.1.: The logic of a photo identity parade

	Suspect is not the perpetrator	Suspect is the perpetrator
Eyewitness has perfect memory	Refusal to select any picture	Selection of target picture
Eyewitness has imperfect memory	Refusal to select any picture, or chance selection of pictures	Refusal to select any picture, or chance selection of pictures

According to Table 1.1 the selection of a suspect's picture in a photo identity parade by all or almost all eyewitnesses implies simultaneously that the suspect is guilty, and that the eyewitnesses have a good memory. It is not necessary to prove that the witnesses have a good memory by means of another independent test: agreement among witnesses is a sufficient proof of their reliability. Hence an identity parade can be used both as a proof of guilt, and as a proof of eyewitness reliability.

The logic seems plausible enough. Naturally a mistake will be made when the suspect is not the wanted criminal but looks *exactly* like him. Hence, in principle, an identification parade cannot prove identity, but only similarity of appearance. Exact equality of appearance is rare. But the difficulty also arises in cases of less perfect likeness, as is best illustrated by the following case (see Buckhout, 1974).

Two men by the names of Lawrence Berson and George Morales were convicted for rape and robbery, respectively. In both cases the real criminal appeared to be a man named Richard Carbone. Both men had denied their guilt, but both were convicted on the basis of identification by eyewitnesses who were absolutely certain. The portraits of the three men

Figure 1.2: Photographs of L. Berson, R. Carbone, and G. Morales.
Mistaken identifications led to the arrests of two innocent men:
Lawrence Berson (left) for several rapes and George Morales (right) for
a robbery. Both men were picked out of police lineups by victims of the
crimes. Berson was cleared when Richard Carbone (center) was arrested
and implicated in the rapes. Carbone was convicted. Later he confessed
to the robbery, clearing Morales. NYT Pictures.

are shown in Figure 1.2. There are clearly three different
people, but the common features are obvious. All three
have black curly hair, glasses, and a little moustache. All
three have a more or less Latin-American appearance. Now
imagine, just for the sake of illustration, that the witnesses
had an imperfect visual memory of the perpetrator's face,
but remembered these characteristics: black curly hair,
glasses, moustache, Latin-American type. Also assume that
poor Berson and Morales were the only ones in the identity
parades who fitted this description. In that case the witnesses
might have refused to point at any person in the lineup, if
they were not sufficiently certain. But once they overcame
their hesitation they would all have selected the same
person, namely the only one who fitted the description.

The occurrence of such close resemblances as demonstrated in Figure 1.2 may be exceptional, which suggests
that in most cases the logic of identity parades will be acceptable. But this suggestion would be wrong: The logic
becomes problematic when it is assumed that witnesses may
have a less than perfect memory, and that they will be
prepared to point at a suspect that bears only a superficial
resemblance to the perpetrator. In such cases the positive
identification does neither prove guilt of the suspect, nor
the reliability of the witnesses. The dual purpose of the
identity parade can only be saved when it is certain that
witnesses with imperfect memories had no special reason to
select the suspect instead of the foils. Such certainty should

be established through painstakingly meticulous procedures with respect to selection of foils, instruction of witnesses, avoidance of suggestion by the investigators, avoidance of contacts among witnesses, etc. The dual objective of identification tests cannot be achieved when such procedures are not strictly followed. The whole logic presented in Table 1.1 will fall through. In any trial in which identification by eyewitnesses is at stake, the prosecution has the obligation to prove that all procedural safeguards, protecting the suspect against mistaken identification, were taken. Desirable safeguards have never been enumerated in an exhaustive list, which makes it sometimes difficult for police investigators to avoid mistakes. The only official investigation of identification procedures that has come to my attention is the Devlin Report (1976), prepared by a special committee appointed by the British Government and presided over by the Right Honorable Lord Devlin. This report provides a limited number of rules, but stresses that no list could ever be complete, and that the court can only protect the falsely accused by increasing the burden of proof. The main theme of this book is a detailed analysis of the procedural safeguards that are needed to guarantee that the dual objectives of identification tests can be achieved. The case of Ivan provides a good illustration of the extreme complexity of this problem.

Although identifications should simultaneously prove the guilt of a suspect and the reliability of the witnesses, they may in fact result from unreliable witnesses falsely recognizing innocent people. In Chapter 2 I will argue that no aspect of eyewitness testimony can be used to distinguish between these two situations. Sometimes this dilemma is solved by acceptance of the assumption that the witnesses are reliable anyway. Such an assumption can be founded on the consideration that the witnesses appeared to be reliable with respect to other aspects of their testimony, that they had a very good opportunity to view the perpetrator, that the experience was too intense to be forgotten, that they declared to see the scene right now (or in their dreams) as vividly as when it happened, that they expressed a high level of confidence, that the identification was corroborated by testimonies from many other subjects, etc. Such *a priori* belief in the reliability of the witnesses may be used as an excuse for the acceptance of flaws in the identification procedures. But even when the procedures are beyond critique one may wonder about the logic of identification tests in such cases. It is highly paradoxical to test the memory of witnesses critically, when for the interpretation of the results it must be assumed in advance that mistakes are impossible. On the contrary, it is logical to assume that reliability is doubted as soon as the police revert to identification tests. The dual objectives of the test can then be achieved only through meticulous procedures. The remaining part of this chapter contains illustrations of the dangers entailed in the prior acceptance of eyewitness reliability.

This problem becomes acute when the reason why suspects are included in identification parades is the very fact that they look like the perpetrator, and not something like possession of the murder weapon, leaving behind clothing, or the presence of a motive. This can easily happen when one of the witnesses discovers the identity of a suspect by leafing through a collection of mugshots in a police station A witness who has some accurate information on the perpetrator's appearance will select suspects from a mugfile who look a bit like the real criminal. Other witnesses, taking part in a subsequent identity parade, are faced with an identity parade in which the suspect bears at least a reasonable degree of resemblance to the perpetrator. They are now expected to have a preference for pointing at the suspect, simply because the person is suspected on the basis of similarity. The reason why the first witness selects a picture from the mugfile is exactly the same reason why subsequent witnesses reveal a preference in the identity parade. When people look so much alike as the three men in Buckhout's example, the only thing that can be established through an identity parade is a resemblance between the suspect and the perpetrator. The term identity parade is a misnomer. It would be better to call it a 'resemblance parade'. When the resemblance was the very reason why the suspect was included in the parade, the parade could as well be omitted, since it confirms only a matter that was known from the beginning. Placing suspects in identity parades after they have been spotted on the basis of search through mugfiles, puts at greatest risk those people whose photographs are for one or another reason at the disposal of the police. This seems an undesirable situation.

The problem of strong resemblance becomes even more pressing when the suspect is the only person in the lineup who fits the description of the criminal. When the witnesses remember a description like 'black curly hair, glasses, moustache, Latin-American type', this should indicate that a lineup of people who all fit this description should be set up. Deviation from this principle creates what is called an unfair lineup. Unfair lineups occur not only through negligence of the investigators, but also when witnesses are unable to verbalize their memories.

It is possible that Buckout's example is exceptional, and that in most cases the logic presented in Table 1.1 is sound and reliable. Two problems are relevant in this context. How much alike can different people be? And how much resemblance is needed to confuse witnesses? Neither of the two questions has been studied beyond the anecdotal. Buckout's case is a good example of close resemblance among people. The case of Mr. Virag illustrates how little resemblance between people is needed to confuse witnesses.

THE CASE OF MR. VIRAG

In July 1969 Laszlo Virag was convicted of offenses committed in Liverpool and Bristol. The offenses in each place consisted of the theft of parking meter coin boxes, involving the use of a firearm, and the wounding of a police officer. He was sentenced to ten years imprisonment in all. In 1974 Mr. Virag was pardoned and released because it became evident that the crimes were committed by someone else, probably a man known as George Payen. The evidence against Mr. Virag consisted of eyewitness testimony only. The case is extensively discussed in the Devlin report.

The Liverpool offense occurred on a Sunday night in

January 1969. Police Constables Callon and Roberts were driving a police car through the center of Liverpool when they saw a man walking in the street, who appeared to have something concealed under his clothes. They told him to stop, but he did not obey this order. Callon then got out of the car and walked after him. When he was about 3 meters away the man turned to face him, brought out a revolver, pointed it at Callon and told him to go away. Callon was almost immediately joined by Roberts. They remained where they were, while the man backed towards a stationary Triumph car. He got into it and drove away. Both policemen declared that they saw his face in full light. Later it appeared that the man had opened two parking meter cash boxes with a home-made key.

The Bristol offense was more complicated. On 23 February 1969 Mr. Cunliffe observed a man opening parking meters. He asked him what he was doing. The man replied that he was from the council and just checking. Cunliffe was suspicious and followed the man through three streets, till he got into a Triumph car. Mr. Cunliffe decided to take the license number, but while doing this he saw a gun being pointed directly at him. He turned round, ran away as fast as he could, and telephoned the police. Police Constables Smith and Organ spotted the Triumph on the M4 motorway. After a complicated chase the criminal left his car and fired several times at the policemen. He hit Smith in the arm, and shouted that he would pay a thousand pounds if they let him go. As a result of this the policemen noticed his mid-European accent. Later on the policemen were assisted by Constables Davies and Bragg. The criminal stopped a Morris 1100 driving along the M4. He got in and told the driver, Mr. Bullock, to drive away as fast as he could, threatening him with the gun. After three miles he switched to another car, driven by Mr. Butcher. Again the criminal used his gun as a threat, and told Mr. Butcher to drive him to Bath, about 30 minutes away. On the journey they had some conversation. In Bath the man took a taxi to Chippenham, driven by Mr. Tucker. In Chippenham he entered the Bear Hotel, where he talked to the hotel manager, Mr. Randall. From there he took a taxi to Newbury, driven by

Mr. Gingell, and another taxi to Reading, driven by Mr. Froom. Then his trail was lost.

The police had only one clue to go upon: the mid-European accent. Almost from the start the police thought that the criminal was most likely a Hungarian, since it was known that some convicted Hungarians were involved in thefts from parking meters. An album was compiled, containing 76 photographs of Hungarians who had Criminal Record Office files. The witnesses Tucker, Randall and Froom picked out Virag, while Gingell picked out another man. On the basis of this result it was decided to stage a live identity parade. Eight witnesses identified Mr. Virag: Police Constables Callon, Roberts, Smith, Davies, and Bragg. He was also identified by Messrs. Tucker, Randall, and Gingell. But many others did not identify Virag, among them: Police Constable Organ, and Messrs. Cunliffe, Bullock, Butcher, and Froom. On the basis of this evidence, and this evidence alone, Mr. Virag was found guilty.

Two years later, in July 1971, a large number of articles associated with the Bristol crime were found in the house of George Payen, an Ukrainian whose real name was Roman Ohorodnyckyi. Among these articles was the gun with which Smith was shot. The fingerprints on the Bristol parking meter cash containers were those of Payen. But the Chief Constable of Gloucestershire pointed out that Virag had been identified by eight witnesses, and that the two men were 'in no way similar in appearance, and that it was therefore difficult to believe that all these witnesses could have been mistaken' (Devlin Report, p. 55). Only in 1974, three years after the discovery of Payen, Mr. Virag was pardoned and released from prison. He was paid £17,500 in compensation for his wrongful conviction and its consequences.

Pictures of Mr. Virag and George Payen are presented in Figure 1.3. They are not very similar. It is miraculous that some of the witnesses recognized Virag after a prolonged confrontation with Payen. It is even more miraculous that the Court neglected the fact that Mr. Cunliffe did *not* recognize Virag. Cunliffe had followed the criminal in the streets of Bristol, and was threatened by him with a gun. Neither

LASZLO VIRAG   GEORGES PAYEN

Figure 1.3: Photographs of L. Virag and G. Payen.

did Mr. Bullock recognize Virag. Bullock had driven the criminal in his Morris 1100, while being threatened by a gun. Mr. Butcher also did not recognize Virag. Butcher had driven the criminal in his taxi for about 30 minutes. Furthermore, Mr. Froom did not recognize Virag, despite having driven the criminal from Newbury to Reading, a distance of 17 miles. It seems as if the Court attached more weight to the positive identifications than to the failures to identify. This reveals another weakness of the identity parade logic. Incorrect identifications, and refusals to point at anyone because of too much uncertainty, can be interpreted as inaccurate memory on the part of the witness. But how do we interpret the positive statement that the criminal is not in the lineup? It does not logically imply a perfect memory, and the procedure does not guarantee that witnesses making such statements are accurate. Hence a judge cannot accept such statements as a proof of innocence. A positive statement that this is *not* the criminal is therefore likely to be neglected. The case of Mr. Virag illustrates clearly that mistaken identity is not dependent upon a close resemblance between people. It was sufficient for the witnesses to register or remember a limited set of features of Payen, and to recognize this limited set in the features of Virag. The extent of this phenomenon can only be estimated when we have a look at the foils used in the identity parade. Unfortunately nothing is known about these foils. It is possible that the foils did not look like either of the two, so that indeed Mr. Virag looked more like the criminal than any of the others. Of course it is not the witnesses' task to judge who *looks most* like the criminal, but whether one of the persons in the lineup *is* the criminal. When the witnesses are convinced that the culprit is in the lineup, they will confuse these two definitions of their task, because in their view the person who looks most like the culprit *is* the culprit. All these problems and many more will return in the case of John Demjanjuk.

A reason why the witnesses were at fault in the case of Mr. Virag was that they were exposed to his face only for a short while, and that he did not behave as a criminal towards all of them. In the case of Ivan the witnesses had seen the criminal many times. Moreover they knew him as a mass murderer. That these conditions still do not exclude mistakes is demonstrated by the case of Frank Walus.

THE CASE OF FRANK WALUS

In 1978 Frank Walus was suspected of committing numerous crimes and atrocities against innocent civilians in the towns of Czestochowa and Kielce, Poland, during the years 1939 to 1943. He would have committed these crimes as a German SS-trooper, and as a member of the Gestapo, the German secret state police. In 1978 Walus was living in the United States under the name of Wallace, and the objective of the prosecution was to revoke his American citizenship on the ground that he did not truthfully answer crucial questions posed to him in 1970, when he applied for citizenship. Walus was identified by 11 different witnesses. They had seen him in the Gestapo Headquarters, they had seen him commit atrocities and outright murders, they had heard him being called 'Herr Walus'. With these 11 witnesses the prosecutor's case looked very strong. As an illustration of the force of these testimonies, three of them will be presented with some more detail. The description of this case is based on the transcripts of the trial that took place in Chicago in 1978 (United States v. Walus).

David Gelbhauer lived in Czestochowa when the Germans occupied Poland in September 1939. He was forced to work inside the Gestapo Headquarters between 1939 and 1943. During that time he witnessed how people were being beaten up or tortured by Walus in the interrogation room. In 1942 Gelbhauer was assigned the job of transporting corpses from the Jewish ghetto to a mass grave. At the site of the grave he saw Walus kill a mother and her two children. He also saw Walus shoot a member of the Polish resistance. He met with Walus almost daily for a period of three and a half years, and Walus talked to him hundreds of times. At the same time he avoided Walus as much as he could, to the extent that he could not describe the color of his eyes, or any other details such as scars. He was shown a set of eight photographs, representing different people suspected of war crimes. Gelbhauer recognized number 7, an undisputed picture of the defendant, but added: 'There is a big difference. He was younger. It is difficult to recognize him.'

Joseph Koenigsberg was also a citizen of Czestochowa who worked in the Gestapo Headquarters for about three weeks. He testified that Frank Walus entered his house and beat up his father. Neighbours then told him that this person's name was Walus Frank, Frank being the family name. Later he was told to polish Walus's boots, and at that occasion Walus talked to him. In 1942 Koenigsberg was a witness to the liquidation of the Czestochowa ghetto. Walus was involved in the selection of those who would be sent to Treblinka, and Koenigsberg witnessed from nearby how Walus shot a Jewish lawyer. Koenigsberg found no difficulty in recognizing Walus from the photospread. He said: 'I will never forget that face. This is the face [of a man] who killed an innocent man whose only crime was the fact that he was a Jew.' As an aside it should be noted that Koenigsberg was requested to identify in the photospread 'any people he knew', although he responded to an advertisement asking for people who had known the war criminal Frank Walus.

Anna Kremski lived in the ghetto of Czestochowa. She was in bed on a Sunday morning in 1942 when the door was opened and a man burst in with a gun in his hand. He pointed the gun at Mrs. Kremski's husband. In one way or another she succeeded in pushing him out. He then ran upstairs and killed an old man. Later she saw the same man many times in German uniform, walking through the streets of the ghetto.

The first time she was interviewed about the incident was in 1976, in a hotel in Tel Aviv. She saw some friends from Czestochowa sitting in the lobby, and went over to join them. One person sitting at the same table asked her: 'Are you born in Czestochowa, do you know a man of this name, Walus?' She answered that she did not. Then, still in the hotel lobby, she was shown pictures, and she recognized the murderer. Later, during the official investigation at the Immigration Service in New York, she was given a different set of pictures, but probably with the same picture of Walus in it. Again she identified Walus's picture, but she never knew the correct name. In fact she testified that she knew this man by the name of Wacusz.

Frank Walus was found guilty of the charges, and his citizenship was taken away from him. But when he appealed, it was decided that Judge Hoffman had made serious mistakes. The evidence showed that the German wartime administrative documentation did not contain any reference to an SS-trooper by the name of Frank Walus. No document existed relating a Frank, Franz, or Franciszek Walus to any German military organization. The Polish war crimes commissions working in Kielce and Czestochowa had no Frank Walus in their records, neither as German military, nor as a collaborator. Walus submitted as an alibi that he was sent from Poland to Bavaria to do forced labor on farms. This was substantiated by several documents, both from German sources and from the International Red Cross. Photos, undisputedly from that time, showed him with the German farmers. The Bavarian families who had known him were found, and they testified that Franz Walus was indeed on their farms during that period of the war. The pictures show him as a very young man, which led Judge Hoffman to suspect that they were pictures of another person. However, there was also an indisputable picture of Walus taken in 1945, showing him as a Civilian Guard in the American occupation forces. The picture shows the same young man. The Appeals Court revoked Judge Hoffman's judgment, and decided that the District Court could try the case again, but that all available evidence had to be taken into account. The case was never reopened, and Frank Walus regained his citizenship. The United States District Court admitted that a serious mistake had been made, that Frank Walus was not the criminal the witnesses knew from 35 years ago, and that Walus should receive compensation. The last recommendation was never followed. In the following we will assume that the Appeals Court and the District Court were correct, and that indeed Frank Walus was not the 'Butcher of Kielce and Czestochowa'.

The investigations into Walus were performed by some of the same people who investigated John Demjanjuk, his picture even appeared in one of the photospreads shown to the witnesses in the Walus case. But apart from these connections there is a larger set of problems to be found in both cases.

The most important problem is the possibility that the suspect is not the perpetrator, but looks like him, and that the witnesses were misled by this resemblance. The test procedure should be such that the likelihood of this error is reduced as much as possible. There is no doubt that the witnesses in the Walus case had a true memory of a person who committed many crimes. It is also likely that this person looked a bit like the older Walus. Probably the young Walus bore less resemblance to the criminal, for instance because he was smaller and much skinnier. It was an unfortunate coincidence that this other person's family name was Frank, Walus, Wacusz, Wacek or Waclaw (all these names were mentioned). As explained before, an identification parade cannot provide absolute guarantees against such mistakes, but at least it could have been tried to render the procedure as safe as possible. It was not.

The specific problems in the Walus case were manifold. The number and the intensity of the confrontations between the witnesses and the criminal were variable. But even Gelbhauer, who had met with him hundreds of times, said that he managed not to look into his eyes during all these years. He had also never seen him without a hat or a cap, not even inside the Gestapo headquarters. None of the witnesses could be specific about his height, not even Izchak Sternberg, a professional tailor.

The issue of the number and intensity of confrontations is central, because it determines whether an identity parade is suitable. Assume that you see your neighbor commit a violent crime when you look out of your window in the middle of the night. You call the police. They pick up your neighbor and place him in a lineup with other people. Your task is to identify the criminal. Since you have known your neighbor for many years, you do not have the slightest problem in identifying him. But is an identity parade really needed to prove that you recognize your neighbor? Could that not be established in a one-person lineup? Many witnesses had seen Walus over and over again. They declared that they knew his face well, and that they would recognize it everywhere. Is an identity parade under such conditions not superfluous and irrelevant? The difference between the direct and immediate recognition of people you know well, and the identification of people on the basis of some features you remembered after a single confrontation is the topic of the following discussion. The lawyer is Mr. Korenkiewicz, the judge is Judge Hoffman.

LAWYER: Mr. Gelbhauer, what is it . . . what is characteristic about the face of the person you have identified in the picture No. 7 that allows you to say today that that is the one and the same person that you saw in Czestochowa during the war and have identified as Mr. Frank Walus?

GELBHAUER: I know the man so well and at that time I really did not go in to look . . . to look at certain details. Generally, I looked at the picture and I saw the face, which I knew so well, and recognized it as the face of Frank Walus.

LAWYER: Your Honor, I do not believe that is responsive to my question and I move. . . .

THE COURT: Oh, I think it is a very intelligent answer. Let me tell you why.

I have seen you on three occasions before. And if you ask me the same question you asked the witness, what is there about your characteristics that make me know you are the same attorney for the defendant who was in here on two or three prior occasions, I could not tell you. And the same thing would apply to you if you were being asked about me. I sustain the . . . rather, I overrule your objection . . . if you move to strike the answer I deny the motion.

LAWYER: I just wonder what the case would be, Your Honor, if you were called upon yourself to identify an attorney you had seen for the last time 35 years ago.

THE COURT: I would only say that I would recognize you any place I saw you as you. But I am not an expert in identification and neither has this witness been offered as an expert in identification. Clearly any human being can . . . may, rather, under oath testify as to whether he saw a certain individual at a given place and time.

LAWYER: I think it is also relevant to determine why he can recognize that person later, what characteristic about a face that exists that would allow him to say that this, among all other persons, is one and the same person.

THE COURT: Most people do not have any special characteristics. I do not think it is fair to a witness, who is willing to hold up his hand to God and swear that he is going to tell the truth, the whole truth, and nothing but the truth, to ask him what I regard as an absurd question. I do not mean that in an offensive way, but I think that is carrying identification by a layman to an absurd extent. (United States of America v. Walus, pp. 233–35)

Clearly the discussants support two different theories of recognition. Judge Hoffman believes that recognition of other people, once you have seen them frequently enough, is immediate. It is like a template, preserved in memory and left undisturbed across any period of time, which matches the appearance of a suspect. The witness can only report that the matching occurred. A reference to special characteristics that determined the recognition cannot be made: it is the face as a whole which is recognized.

Lawyer Korenkiewicz believes that recognition is based upon the comparison of a limited set of features. The probability of a mistake increases when the number of features is getting too small, or when features are used that are shared by many people. Therefore he wants to know what these features were in the case of Frank Walus. Recognition on the basis of an immediate global matching seems the more natural description when the task is to recognize one's neighbor. Comparison of features seems more plausible when the task is to recognize a person whose outward appearance is not clearly impressed upon one's memory. Which of the two was the most likely in the cases of Frank Walus and John Demjanjuk? We will have more to say about this problem in the following chapters.

A second problem is the long retention period. This is a dual disadvantage. Not only may the memory of the witnesses have faded, but also the perpetrator will have changed too much to stage a fair live lineup. One must resort to photos, and there is no guarantee that suitable photos will be available. In the case of Walus the investigators could not use a picture taken during the war, and when such a picture became available in the course of the trial its authenticity was challenged. This introduces the question how much an older person can look like another person, when that other person was young. Can a person change so much that he now resembles the remembered face of another young person much more than he resembles himself when young?

A third problem is the construction of the photo parade. Which other pictures go into it? Probably Judge Hoffman would have argued that this is irrelevant. Once you recognize a person, it is immaterial what the other portraits look like. Lawyer Korenkiewicz would object that the question is highly relevant. If the witnesses remember just a few features, like round face and receding chin, and none of the other people portrayed share this combination of features, then it could happen that witnesses selected the suspect's picture just for this reason. In the cross examination 12 witnesses were asked to remember distinguishing features. Only some very general characteristics were mentioned: strong build, medium size, brown hair, age a little over 20. Nothing much to go by, nothing related to Walus's face, and definitely not enough to guarantee that the lineup was not blatantly unfair. One indication about the haphazard composition of the lineup can be obtained from the fact that the picture of John Demjanjuk, who does not at all look like Walus, served as a foil in the photospread. One puts little trust in the memory of witnesses, if one assumes that they could confuse the rather small and skinny Walus with the giant Demjanjuk.

A fourth problem is the control of the test situation. How are the witnesses instructed? It is generally agreed that witnesses should be explicitly advised that perhaps the criminal's picture is not in the set. The pictures should be placed before the witness in such a way that no one picture is emphasized more than the others. But how are such things done in the lobby of an hotel in Tel Aviv, when witnesses are interviewed in the presence of old friends, rather than a lawyer? How do we know that the investigators, who know which picture is the suspect's, do not unconsciously influence the witnesses' choices? Again Judge Hoffman might argue that this danger is nonexistent when one recognizes a highly familiar person. But how well did Anna Kremsky know Walus? She had seen him a few seconds in her own house, and afterwards only in the streets of Czestochowa, where the SS-trooper was wearing a cap, and where Anna tried to avoid him as much as possible.

A fifth problem is the repeated presentation of photospreads. Anna Kremski was shown a limited set of pictures in the hotel lobby. She identified Frank Walus. Later, in the offices of the Immigration Service in New York, she was shown a larger set of pictures, probably because the investigators suspected that the choice from the small set was too easy. Again she recognized Walus, but why? Because she remembered his face from 35 years ago, or because she had seen exactly the same picture six months ago? The same problem arises when a witness is asked to identify a suspect in the courtroom after having seen a picture of the same person. This happened systematically in the Walus case.

STATE ATTORNEY: Mr. Gelbhauer, at this time do you see in the courtroom the man Frank Walus whom you have testified about here today? (U.S. of America v. Walus, p. 110)

STATE ATTORNEY: Now Mr. Koenigsberg, the man that you saw in your apartment, and the man you saw in the Gestapo Headquarters, and the man you later saw at the liquidation, the man that you knew as Frank Walus, is he here in this courtroom today? (U.S. of America v. Walus, p. 259)

STATE ATTORNEY: I would like you to look around the courtroom and see anyone you recognize?

ANNA KREMSKI: That is the man (pointing). That is the man. (U.S. of America v. Walus, p. 786)

Similar questions were asked of all witnesses. Of course Frank Walus was seated in the dock, which made the answer very easy. But apart from that, even when the witnesses believed sincerely that they recognized Walus, the question still remains as to whether they recognized him because they had seen his picture before.

A sixth problem is that many witnesses responded with great certainty, although, as we now know, they were wrong. Judge Hoffman might have picked up this aspect, because it could indicate the type of immediate recognition he was expecting. But apparently certainty on the part of the witnesses does not exclude errors. Is there any useful information in the fact that witnesses are certain?

A final problem is that of the missed identifications. Out of the 12 eyewitnesses presented in the Walus case only one had failed to make a positive identification during official hearings. But it is not at all clear how many other people attempted identification in hotel lobbies or other unofficial places, in preparation for official hearings. If witnesses are selected on the basis of their tendency to point at the suspect's photograph, it is not surprising that a considerable concordance among witnesses is achieved. Prosecutors are not obliged to provide such information, defending lawyers do not care to ask the question, probably because they would not receive an answer anyway. Judge Hoffman was faced with the almost impossible task of discarding 11 witnesses in order to arrive at the correct conclusion, without knowing that possibly the eleven witnesses formed a minority.

THE CASE OF MARINUS DE RIJKE

The preceding discussion is troubled by one issue that raises many emotions: whether survivors of Nazi camps will forget some aspects of their experiences in the course of 35 years. One could argue that these experiences were too horrible to be forgotten, and that every detail, including the faces of the perpetrators, are engraved upon the minds of those who survived. In that case the problem of identifying Ivan simply does not occur. But there are a number of reasons why such an extreme reliance on the memory of surviving witnesses could be challenged. The obvious problems in the Walus case constitute one of those reasons. There have been no studies into the reliability of the memories of concentration camp survivors after 35 years in a systematic way. The only exception is my own study of the case of Marinus De Rijke (Wagenaar and Groeneweg, 1988).

Marinus De Rijke served as an Oberkapo in the penal colony Camp Erika in The Netherlands during the years 1942 and 1943. The colony was used for common criminals convicted in Dutch courts for ordinary misdemeanors and crimes. But the commanders of the camp had initiated a German-type regime, complete with excessive punishments and torture, often resulting in death. Most of the dirty work was left to Kapos and Oberkapos, prisoners who obtained certain privileges by maintaining discipline among their fellows. De Rijke was one of them, and he became notorious for his criminal conduct, which went far beyond what was expected of Kapos. In 1943 the camp was closed when the Dutch authorities learned what had happened. Immediately thereafter the police started interviewing the survivors. Among them was a group that consisted originally of a thousand prisoners who were sent to Germany for forced labor. Six hundred of these people died under the hands of their Kapos, not through German brutality. Finally the remainder of the group were sent back to Camp Erika, because they had become too weak. Many of these 400 died after they returned to the camp, again through the bestial treatment they received from the Kapos, their fellow countrymen. The survivors are not wholly comparable with the survivors of Treblinka, but it is eminently clear that their lives had also been directly threatened over a long period of time. The special feature of the De Rijke case is that some witnesses were interviewed in the 1940s and again 40 years later, when De Rijke was tried in court. This made it possible to compare the statements made shortly after the events, and the recollections after 40 years.

A total of 140 statements were obtained from 78 different witnesses. Twenty-two witnesses were interrogated between 1943 and 1948; fifteen of those were also interrogated after 1984. Most of the interviews were haphazard and unsystematic. Hence the number of answers varies from one question to the other. A more complete analysis of all these statements is presented elsewhere (Wagenaar & Groeneweg, 1988). Here follows a summary.

Of 38 witnesses who reported that they had been maltreated or tortured by De Rijke, three had forgotten his name after 40 years. One of those three was also interrogated in 1947, and on that occasion he knew the name quite well.

The witnesses who were interrogated in both periods reproduced 48 names of guards and Kapos in the first period. After 40 years they could only reproduce 19 of these names.

A picture of De Rijke taken in the camp was shown to 55 witnesses. Forty-one witnesses said they recognized him, but 14 did not, although it is certain that all of them had known De Rijke. This score is probably somewhat inflated, since the same picture had already been shown on a nation-wide television broadcast. Thirty-seven of the witnesses who were confronted with the photo were also asked whether they had seen the television program. The answers to this question are presented in Table 1.2. The result suggests that recognition was influenced by watching the television program.

Table 1.2: The recognition of De Rijke's picture after seeing or not seeing the television broadcast

	Recognized	Not recognized
Seen TV program	20	5
Not seen TV program	7	5

The interaction is not statistically significant, but that is not essential. The real point is that of the twelve witnesses who did not watch the television program only 58 per cent recognized De Rijke. In Chapter 2 I will explain that this is the recognition rate which should be expected when in fact no witness had actually seen De Rijke before.

It is generally believed that being a victim in the hands of a torturer will contribute to the later recognition of the criminal. Some pertinent data are shown in Table 1.3.

Table 1.3: The recognition of De Rijke's picture after having been maltreated by him

	Recognized	Not recognized
Maltreated	24	6
Not maltreated	14	5

Of those who were maltreated or tortured by De Rijke, 80 per cent recognized his picture, which is not significantly different from recognition score of 74 percent for those who were not maltreated. Hence, being maltreated by a person did not promote recognition after 40 years.

In 59 cases witnesses mentioned the date on which they entered the camp. The accuracy within two groups is reported in Table 1.4.

Table 1.4: The recall of the date on which witnesses entered Camp Erika

	Error less than one month	Error one month or more
Reports between 1943 and 1948	9	2
Reports between 1984 and 1988	8	11

The interaction is statistically significant. After 40 years there were three witnesses who erred by approximately six months. Hence they situated their arrival in the wrong season. One witness said literally: 'It was not quite winter, but late fall; hence it must have been November or December.' In reality he arrived in July!

A comparison of the statements made by those 15 witnesses who testified in both periods 1943–48 and 1984–88 reveals some remarkable instances of forgetfulness. The names of the witnesses are abbreviated, as is customary in The Netherlands.

Witness C. reported how a prisoner died in his crib. De Rijke and another guard by the name of Boxmeer came in, and dragged away the body in a most repulsive manner. By 1984 he had forgotten the event, and De Rijke.

Witness Van D. was maltreated by a guard named Daalhuizen, to such an extent that he was unable to do any work for a full year. By 1984 he had forgotten the name of Daalhuizen.

Witness H. saw how a fellow prisoner was maltreated by De Rijke and Boxmeer so that he died. By 1984 he had forgotten both names. In 1943 he reported how another prisoner De V. was violently assaulted by Boxmeer. In 1984 he reported that De V. was the perpetrator instead of the victim!

Witness Van der M. was beaten up by De Rijke, and was unable to walk for several days. In 1984 he only remembered receiving an occasional kick. He also witnessed the killing of a Jewish fellow prisoner, but had forgotten all about it by 1984.

Witness S. reported that the guards Diepgrond and Boxmeer had drowned a prisoner in a water trough. He did not remember this in 1984, and even denied having said it.

Finally witness Van de W. was maltreated by De Rijke, but in 1984 he systematically called him De Bruin. He did not recall his own maltreatment, neither did he remember seeing how some Jewish prisoners were beaten to death with a whip.

All these memory failures do not mean that concentration camp survivors forget what has happened. Almost all survivors could provide mutually consistent global accounts, and even the large majority of reproduced details were correct. When they erred, they were rarely completely wrong. However, it cannot be denied that discrepancies between early and late testimonies were observed in 10 out of the 15 cases for which two testimonies were available. The horror of the events, the intensity of the emotions felt at the time and ever since, are no warrant against forgetting or confounding of details. One should not be dogmatic about the memories of concentration camp survivors.

Another lesson learned from the case of Marinus De Rijke is that recognition of a photo is meaningless when the photo is not presented within a larger spread of foils. By presenting the witnesses with one picture only, the investigators fully destroyed the already shaky logic of the identity parade. The reason why the picture was shown at all was that the investigators wanted to establish that the witnesses did not confound De Rijke with another guard. Hence the question was not 'Can they identify De Rijke as one of their guards?' but 'Can they identify De Rijke among other guards?' An answer to the first question could be obtained by placing De Rijke's picture amongst the pictures of innocent foils. The second question can only be answered when De Rijke's picture is placed amongst the pictures of other guards. The presentation of a single picture enabled witnesses to answer the first question, while the investigators assumed they were answering the second.

IS THERE A MEMORY PROBLEM?

The identification of Ivan is only problematic when it is agreed that surviving witnesses might experience a memory problem. Otherwise we must simply accept the available testimonies. The cases presented above suggest that such a problem might indeed exist. But a superficial look at the testimonies in the Demjanjuk case makes it clear that the recognition test presented at least some of the witnesses with a serious problem. Consider that not all witnesses made a positive identification, and that some witnesses made a positive identification in one test, but failed to do so in another test. Consider that some witnesses needed a considerable time before they were able to make a choice. And consider that some witnesses expressed a substantial degree of uncertainty. None of this suggests that recognition was immediate and easy.

However, that recognition is difficult does not mean that all witnesses were at fault. In the end the five witnesses who testified in the Jerusalem court were absolutely certain that John Demjanjuk was Ivan. It is not known how serious their memory problems were, nor whether these problems could have led them into error. Even worse: we will probably never know the extent of the memory problem, because we will probably never know the truth in this case.

We can only look at the extent to which the identification parade proved that John Demjanjuk was Ivan the Terrible of Treblinka. It is clear now that an identity parade could not provide absolute proof. But is the identity proved beyond doubt? In order to answer that question we must know much more about the psychological processes involved in face recognition. We must identify all task aspects that could enhance or impede the reliability of an identity parade. And most of all, we must scrutinize the procedures used in the investigation against Demjanjuk in order to establish whether such task aspects were present or absent.

Specifically, it should be established that the identity parade was organized such that witnesses without an accurate memory of Ivan's face were unable to select Demjanjuk's picture. And that those who passed the test were not mistaken by a superficial resemblance between John and Ivan.

2 The Reliability of Facial Identifications

The central question in the Demjanjuk case is whether the witnesses were correct when they recognized Ivan in the photospreads presented to them. If the answer is yes, then it implies that John Demjanjuk is the same person as Ivan. This question should be answered by the Court, because no expert can answer it. But an expert on eyewitness identification problems can contribute background information on those variables which affect the reliability of eyewitnesses. This chapter will give such background information, based upon experimental research on recognition reliability. The implications for forensic practice are discussed in Chapter 3. For the sake of continuity I will not refer to the publications in which the supporting research for every single statement can be found. Instead I refer the reader to two recent studies that summarize the available knowledge. One is by Shapiro and Penrod (1986), the other by Cutler, PPenrod and Martens (1987). References to other publications are made only when they do not appear in these two publications. Both studies are concerned with the reliability aspect, not with theories of face recognition. I will follow this emphasis, since a discussion of the various theories of face recognition will not contribute to the understanding of our practical problem.

Before entering a detailed discussion of the factors that affect eyewitness reliability, it should be stressed that reliability studies form a branch of the much older tradition of memory research. Many notions, like the three processing stages, encoding, retention, and reproduction, are simply borrowed from this tradition. However, this does not mean that all results of memory research are relevant to our topic. On the contrary, much memory research focusses on the recall of meaningless material, like lists of letters, numbers, or syllables in a random order. If meaningful material is used, the emphasis is often on verbal material, like stories and news items. The restriction to the studies referenced in Shapiro and Penrod does therefore not impose undue limitations. The literature on face recognition and eyewitness identification is well presented by this sample.

Another characteristic of this chapter is that the presentation is limited to research findings. The underlying theories are omitted, because they have no relevance for the development of the rules that are presented in Chapter 3. In this respect the presentation is rather like a section of expert testimony in court, in which usually the findings are presented without the theories.

PROBLEMS IN THE COMPARISON OF EXPERIMENTAL STUDIES

The study by Shapiro and Penrod (1986) is a meta-analysis of 128 different experimental investigations. The idea of a meta-analysis is to average results across a large number of independent experimental studies. The average result is represented by a quantity called effect size, which indicates how large the effect of a variable is on people's performance, relative to the normal variation that is caused by all uncontrolled influences. The use of effect size instead of statistical significance is especially meaningful for the judgment of practical relevance, because a highly significant effect with a small size will have only a marginal influence on the acceptance of testimony. Take as an example the question of whether witnesses knew at the time of the event that they would be questioned. The effect size of this variable is estimated by combining those studies in the set in which this variable was manipulated. There were five such studies. The effect of advance knowledge that a test will occur on the number of correct identifications (hits) is computed across the available studies, as well as the effect of the number of incorrect identifications (false alarms). The effect of advance knowledge on hits, expressed as a standardized score, was 0.10, which means that the number of hits increased when advance knowledge was given, but the increase was small: only one tenth of the standard deviation. At the same time there was an effect of 0.27 on false alarms, which means that false alarms decreased by about one quarter standard deviation. In some studies actual hit and false alarm rates are published.This happened in two studies on advance knowledge. The combined hit rates for advance knowledge present was 56 percent, for advance knowledge about 58 percent. The combined false alarm rates were 27 percent in both cases. This means that in these two studies no effect of advance knowledge was found.

Some of the variables, such as initial exposure to the target, retention period, or number of foils in the test phase, are continuous rather than dichotomous. That is to say, the contribution of such variables cannot be expressed by a few hit rates and false alarm rates. Shapiro and Penrod solved this problem by presenting these contributions as correlations in a multiple regression analysis. Since the reader is not assumed to understand this statistical procedure, I will refer only to the conclusions that were drawn from it.

HITS AND FALSE ALARMS

Before beginning a discussion of those factors which were found to influence identification performance, I will explain in more detail the logical difficulty of the distinction between hits and false alarms. First I will define target-present lineups as those lineups in which the criminal is present, target-absent lineups as those where the criminal is not present. In target-present lineups, hit rates tell us how often the real criminal is identified, while false alarm rates tell us how often foils are identified as the criminal; that is, how often a foil is judged to look more like the remembered image of the criminal than the criminal himself. But in actual practice a court will not make mistakes when a foil is falsely identified as the perpetrator, simply because the investigators know that foils are innocent. The real concern is that witnesses may identify an innocent suspect, that is, a suspect in a target-absent lineup. The relevant statistic is how often, when the criminal is *not* in the lineup, an innocent suspect is judged to resemble the remembered image of the criminal sufficiently to make a positive response. There is no logical relationship between false alarms in target-present lineups and positive responses in target-absent lineups. Table 2.1 is a schematic presentation of this distinction.

Table 2.1: Interpretation of positive and negative responses, with target present or absent

	Positive response	No positive response
Target-present lineup	hit or false alarm	missed target
Target-absent lineup	false alarm	correct rejection

In a real lineup, involving a suspect and a number of foils, we will always be able to recognize false alarms when a foil is identified as the criminal. Since the suspect is the only possible target, identifications of other people are clearly false alarms. The problem occurs when the suspect is identified: is this a hit in a target-present lineup, or a false alarm in a target-absent lineup? Only 12 studies out of the 128 compared target-present and target-absent lineups. The overall hit rate in target-present studies was typically around 70 percent. The false alarm rate in target-absent studies was 52 percent. If we assume a 50 percent prior probability that the target is present, a positive identification increases the probability of guilt to 70/(70+52) which is only 57 percent. Thus we find that the hit rate in target-present lineups presents an over-optimistic portrayal of the practical reliability of eyewitnesses. An experimental demonstration of this problem is provided by the study of Cutler *et al.* (1987) who obtained the data presented in Table 2.2.

Table 2.2: Experimental results of Cutler, Penrod, and Martens (1987)

	Positive response		No positive response
	Hits	False alarms	
Target-present lineup	43%	52%	5%
Target-absent lineup	–	68%	32%

In this practical situation false alarms in the target-present lineup were detected immediately. In the target-absent lineups the response rate is considerably lower, but the rate of responding to new faces is in fact going up. Most studies on face recognition and eyewitness identification involve only target-present lineups. This is despite the logical truth that false alarm rates in target-present lineups are wholly uninformative, unless one assumes that alarm rates in both target-present and target-absent lineups are determined by the same factors. This is not certain because, as mentioned before, the two errors are psychologically quite different. A false alarm in a target-present lineup occurs when the resemblance between the remembered face and a foil is closer than between the remembered face and the target. This implies almost by necessity that there is something wrong with the memory of the face. A false alarm in a target-absent lineup occurs when a foil sufficiently resembles the face being remembered. For that to happen there need be nothing wrong with the memory. However Cutler *et al.* (1987) reported that choosing rates for target-present and target-absent lineups were affected by exactly the same factors.

From the foregoing discussion it is clear that the diagnostic value of a positive response in an identity parade depends on two different sets of factors; those that increase the correct identification in a target-present lineup, and those that increase the response rate in a target-absent lineup. Both sets will be presented below, with the proviso that, because of the scarcity of research on target-absent lineups, false alarms are considered mostly in the context of target-present lineups.

FACTORS RELATED TO THE WITNESSES

Individual differences with respect to the ability of identifying criminals in lineups appeared to be relatively small. The only important factor was age: children produced 12 percent fewer hits and 10 percent more false alarms than adults. Effect size was only 0.8 standard deviation units. Women produced slightly more hits, and slightly fewer false alarms than men.

A most perplexing factor was training of recognition abilities. Some relatively extensive training procedures did not improve performance, in contrast to some other brief training that appeared to result in positive effects. Probably the decisive factor was not how much training people received, but what was actually taught. Looking at specific facial features, such as nose, eyes, etc., did not generally improve recognition performance, whereas attention to global aspects of a face (honesty, typical Russian, looks like my Uncle Bert) had some beneficial effects. This finding lends some support to Judge Hoffman: a witness attending to global features might identify a criminal correctly, without being able to mention any specific features. On the other hand, it is obvious that attention to global features might still lead to misidentification when an innocent suspect shares these features with the real perpetrator. The aspect of training is relevant for the identification by professional witnesses, such as police officers. The jury in the case of Mr. Virag could have reasoned that the police constables who recognized the suspect had enough professional experience to be reliable witnesses. In fact we now know that experience and most types of special training do not enhance the ability to identify people. Training is of course nonexistent when witnesses are non-professionals, such as the survivors of Treblinka.

In all it can be said that there are no individual characteristics that qualify one group of witnesses better than another.

FACTORS RELATED TO THE TARGETS

Transformation
The most important factor related to the target is a transformation occurring between the encoding and the lineup. Transformations occurred when a criminal used a disguise such as glasses, headgear, wigs, masks, a moustache or a beard. Other transformations were in the pose or expression, a change to photographic stills, or a change of age. The effect of tranformations was a 21 percent decrease of hits, and an 8 percent increase of false alarms in target-present lineups. In the study by Cutler *et al.* (1987) it appeared that witnesses made fewer positive responses when no transformation occurred between the staged robbery and the subsequent lineup. The effect was equally large in target-absent lineups. The relevance of transformation is quite obvious in the case of Demjanjuk, when it is realized that the test differed from the original confrontation in many ways. Stills were shown instead of live people. The picture showed Demjanjuk at the age of 30, nine years older than he would have been in Treblinka. Ivan wore a uniform, Demjanjuk wore civilian clothing.

Distinctiveness
The second important target characteristic is whether the target face was easily distinguishable from all other faces encountered during encoding or test stages. Distinctive features elicited 10 percent more hits, and 12 percent fewer false alarms. The practical value of this finding is unclear because there is no accepted method for the assessment of the distinctiveness of a target's face. Lawyers could argue that their clients are easily confounded with other people because they happen to have an undistinctive face. But such a claim cannot be supported by experimental proof. Whether John Demjanjuk's face is distinctive or not depends on all the other faces which the witnesses had seen during their war experiences. Many Ukrainians may have looked like Demjanjuk. In target-absent lineups distinctiveness could even have the opposite effect: when the suspect is placed in the lineup on the basis of his resemblance to

the criminal, a clear distinction between the suspect and the foils should result in an increased false alarm rate. Face distinctiveness should be the same for all persons in a lineup, suspect and foils, in order to ensure that witnesses will not select the suspect on the basis of distinctiveness alone. The fairness of a lineup in this respect can be tested by using mock witnesses before the actual witnesses are exposed to it.

Perhaps surprisingly, two other aspects of the target face, gender and race, appeared to be relatively unimportant. This meant that the faces of males were not easier to recognize than the faces of females; nor were white faces more distinguishable than black or Asian faces. Difficulties of cross-race identification were reported in many studies, but the effects were not consistent, which is why the effect disappeared in the meta-analysis across studies. Cross-race identification is a much discussed issue, because in actual practice it occurs quite frequently that witnesses of one race claim to recognize suspects of another race, while at the same time many people assume on intuitive grounds that recognizing a person of another race presents special difficulties. Apparently such an effect, if it exists at all, is moderated by a number of other variables. In the present case the issue is of little importance, as there is little reason to believe that Jewish survivors will find it difficult to distinguish their Ukrainian guards because of race differences.

FACTORS RELATED TO ENCODING

Focussing of attention

It appeared that the most important aspect of the encoding stage is the focussing of attention. In facial recognition studies subjects usually inspect a series of pictures, with the explicit instruction to try to remember. In eyewitness studies it is possible to diffuse the attention throughout the scene. It is even possible to let subjects be witnesses to an event while they are unaware of the fact that they are taking part in an experiment. Focussing of attention was a major determinant of identification accuracy, but can, in actual practice, be of little service, since it defies manipulation. We can only attempt to assess the amount of focussing during a crime, and take this assessment into account when reliability becomes the issue.

Instruction

A factor closely related to focussing was the instruction given in facial recognition studies. The instruction could stress attention to distinctive features, or attention to psychological traits of the targets. It appeared that attention to global traits increased the hit rate by 12 percent, while it decreased the false alarm rate by 6 percent. Hit rates were also increased by the addition of verbal descriptions in the study phase, such as 'friendly looking' or 'cool personality'.

Time spent

A set of factors related to the time spent on the encoding of faces were total exposure time, number of targets, and number of other faces presented. Exposure time, which typically varied from a few seconds to one minute did not have a major influence on reliability scores. However, it is obvious that the exposure time in the case of Ivan was of a different order, and it is not surprising that the State Prosecutor tried to found his confidence in the witnesses upon their prolonged confrontation with Ivan. The case of De Rijke demonstrates that even prolonged exposure does not necessarily warrant correct recognition.

Mode, pose, and advance knowledge

Minor aspects of the encoding situation were mode of presentation, pose, and advance knowledge. Mode of presentation refers to the use of stills, videotapes, or live enactments in the encoding stage. This aspect is of little practical interest, since few crimes are actually witnessed by means of stills or video. Presentation of a three-quarter pose led to 12 percent more hits compared to front or profile presentations, but again this factor is not so relevant when the confrontation in an actual crime is long enough. The cases of Mr. Virag, Frank Walus, and Marinus De Rijke, presented in Chapter 1, are clear examples of situations in which pose could not be a decisive factor. Advance knowledge of the future recognition task had no measurable effect. This is somewhat unexpected, because one might assume that witnesses, knowing that they will testify, will pay more attention. The explanation could be that witnesses pay attention to the face of a perpetrator of a crime, or the faces of people encountered in a more artificial situation, even when they do not expect a test. Another explanation could be that witnesses, when they pay extra attention, focus on facial features like shape of nose, eyes, and so on. We have already seen that attention for such details does not improve later recognition. The consequence of this lack of effect is not unimportant. A defense lawyer's statement that witnesses cannot be accurate because at the time of the crime they could not expect to be tested is simply invalid. The reverse, that witnesses will be more accurate, because they anticipated their later testimony, is equally untrue.

FACTORS RELATED TO STORAGE

Retention interval
The retention interval is one of the most frequently studied influences on human memory. The general finding is, of course, that forgetting increases when time passes. But the rate of forgetting is considerably different for various types of material. Meaningless lists of numbers may be forgotten in a few minutes, but nursery rhymes learned in early childhood may stay forever. The retention interval used in typical eyewitnesses identification studies varied from several hours to weeks, and this range appeared to be insufficient for the establishment of large and consistent effects. Cutler *et al.* (1987) even reported a counterintuitive beneficial effect of the longer interval. Obviously the range employed in empirical studies is not at all representative of the retention period in Demjanjuk's case.

Only one experimental study by Bahrick, Bahrick, and Wittlinger (1975) covered a retention interval of over 30 years. The study was on the recognition of classmates in graduation pictures. The surprising conclusion of this study was that classmates can be recognized with an accuracy of between 80 and 90 percent, even after 50 years. There are, however, several problems in this study. The first is that the encoding period was probably very long, much longer than in most criminal cases, even the case of Ivan. The second problem is that all subjects contributed their own graduation pictures, which means that they received a picture that they had seen many times before. Maybe they would find it much more difficult to recognize other pictures of their classmates. The third problem is that the subjects could have peeked at the pictures before handing them in, which would reduce the retention period to almost zero. The fourth problem is that Bahrick *et al.* did not use target-absent lineups as a control. The really intriguing question is how often people will, after 50 years, point at the person who resembles a classmate more than the others, even when the lineup does not contain anyone they have met before. As it stands now, we cannot say that recognition accuracy is systematically related to retention interval, or that a retention interval of 40 years renders recognition impossible. The testimony by 78 witnesses in the case of Marinus de Rijke (see Chapter 1) does not change this position, because of the gross mistakes made by the police investigators.

Post-event information
The second storage factor is information received during the retention period. Presentation of mugshots during the retention interval had an effect in some experimental studies, but little in others. The decisive factor seemed to be whether or not subjects were told that none of the faces seen during the interval belonged to the criminal. Apparently subjects could avoid committing mugshots to memory, if they knew that they were not related to the crime. In practice one must be afraid that intervening confrontations, for instance in the course of a criminal investigation, will decrease recognition accuracy, because witnesses are usually not told to erase such memories. We will see in Chapter 4 that many witnesses in Ivan's case were confronted with Demjanjuk's picture in the course of the investigation against Fedor Fedorenko. This meant that they could have

committed this picture to memory during the retention period.

FACTORS RELATED TO RETRIEVAL

Context reinstatement
The most powerful determinant reported in studies on face recognition and eyewitness identification was reinstatement of the original context. Context reinstatement was achieved by presentation of verbal cues previously associated with the targets or the criminal incident. After context reinstatement the hit rate increased by as much as 25 percent. However, the number of false alarms increased simultaneously by about 5 percent. Enthusiasm for extended employment of context reinstatement is tempered somewhat by the finding that the effect was most pronounced in laboratory studies. In realistic conditions witnesses seemed to rely on a spontaneous re-enactment, even when they were instructed not to do so.

Lineup instructions
Another powerful manipulation is the explicit mention of the option of 'no choice' when nobody resembles the criminal closely enough. Usually one refers to lineup instructions that do not offer the 'no-choice' option in an explicit manner, as *biased* instructions. Malpass and Devine (1981) reported 90 percent positive choices under biased instructions, and 56 percent positive choices under unbiased instructions, both in target-present lineups. In target-absent lineups biased instructions resulted in 78 percent false alarms, while unbiased instructions reduced the false alarm rate to 33 percent. It is obvious that instructions to witnesses should always be explicit about the no-choice option, and that official records should mention an exact account of the instructions as they were given. Identification attempts in hotel lobbies or other informal procedures are highly undesirable because one will tend to relax procedural rigidity, while the exact instructions are not properly documented. In the case of Marinus de Rijke most of the witnesses had

seen a television program in which it was emphasized that the police had discovered a picture of De Rijke in his camp uniform. At the later identification trials they were never advised that the picture possibly represented another person.

Other factors. A group of mutually related aspects has to do with the number of targets and foils in the recognition test. In criminal investigation procedures there is usually only one target in the lineup, whereas the number of foils may vary. In this situation it was found that performance improved as the number of foils increased. The explanation could be that in larger lineups there were often a few candidates who looked like the remembered image of the criminal. The *embarras du choix* helped to make witnesses aware of the fact that their image of the target was not perfectly clear.

Another factor was presentation by stills, video or live lineups. The difference between the recognition rates in these conditions was marginal or nonexistent. This result is counterintuitive, because it is generally assumed that recognition will be easier when more retrieval cues are available. One explanation suggested by Helen Dent of the University of Leeds (1977) is that live lineup confrontations increase the anxiety of witnesses, which counteracts the beneficial effect of increasing the number of retrieval cues.

TARGET-ABSENT LINEUPS AND THE RATE OF CHOOSING

More relevant than any other factor mentioned before was the distinction between target-present and target-absent lineups. The forensic application of eyewitness research does not require studies of target-present lineups, simply because false identifications of foils in target-present identification parades will immediately reveal the unreliability of the witness's memory. It is the false identification of a suspect in a target-absent lineup that causes conviction of the innocent.

The overall hit rate for target-present lineups was between

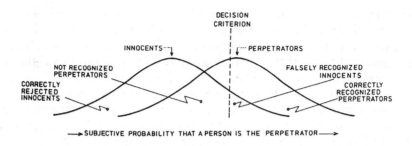

Figure 2.1: The signal detection representation of the choice in target-present and target-absent lineups. For explanation, see text.

70 and 80 percent. But in twelve experiments on target-absent lineups a false alarm rate of 52 percent was reported. Rules and procedures for the conduct of identity parades should be aimed at reducing this number.

The choice between a positive response and rejection of the lineup can be viewed as a signal detection problem. The signal to be detected is the presence of the target in the lineup. The decision to make is whether the resemblance between the most likely participant in the lineup and the remembered image of the criminal is close enough. In order to make this decision the witness needs to adopt a decision criterion: how much resemblance is needed for a positive response? The chosen decision criterion can be conservative, which means that only a high degree of resemblance will lead to a positive identification. A lesser amount of resemblance is required when a more lenient criterion is adopted. The choice between conservative and lenient decision criteria in signal detection problems is, in principle, independent of the difficulty of the decision. Figure 2.1 presents the decision problem graphically. The left-hand curve is a frequency distribution of the likelihoods elicited by non-targets. It shows, in this hypothetical case, that non-targets are rarely likely to be the perpetrator. The right-hand curve represents the targets. They do not always resemble the remembered image, because the image could be incomplete or wrong, but on the whole they are more like the remembered image than non-targets. A positive identification is made when the likelihood of a person being the perpetrator is above the adopted decision criterion, the dotted line in Figure 2.1. There are two areas to the right of this criterion line. One is the tail of the non-target distribution, which represents the non-targets that so strongly resemble the remembered image that they will be taken for the perpetrators. The other is the main body of the target distribution. This part stands for the correctly identified perpetrators. To the left of the decision criterion there are also two areas. One is the tail of the target distribution, which represents the perpetrators who were not recognized. The other is the main body of the non-target distribution, where we find the non-targets who were correctly rejected. A right-hand shift of the decision criterion reduces the frequency of false alarms, but does at the same time increase the number of missed targets. A left-hand shift, towards a more lenient criterion, increases the probability of identifying the target, but simultaneously increases the risk of false alarms. The finding that 52 percent of the witnesses in target-absent lineups make a positive identification, can be represented graphically by shifting the decision criterion in Figure 2.1 to the left, to about the centre of the non-target distribution.

A large body of literature has shown that the location of the decision criterion in signal detection situations is influenced by a number of situational aspects. Malpass and Devine (1984) were the first authors who listed aspects of the eyewitness identification situation that could influence the location of the decision criterion. Five of these aspects are discussed below.

Costs and benefits
The first influence that may elicit a lenient decision criterion is that witnesses desire the conviction and subsequent punishment of the criminal. This is in fact a cost-benefit argument. The benefit of a conviction is large. The subjective cost of the feeling that a criminal has escaped justice might be even larger. The cost of convicting the wrong person is very high according to norms accepted by our

society. But it could be estimated as low by witnesses, especially in a case like Demjanjuk's where many people have told me that, even if he is not Ivan, he certainly is a criminal who has something to hide. The justified acquittal of an innocent suspect is again highly valued by our society, but it is not the main concern of a witness for the prosecution. It is abundantly clear from the literature that the outcome of such a cost-benefit analysis is about the most powerful influence on the choice of a decision criterion. In the case of John Demjanjuk there are two reasons why the cost-benefit argument carries much weight. One is that all witnesses were Treblinka survivors. As we will see in Chapter 4, some of the witnesses declared that their sole motivation to survive was to testify before the world about what happened in Treblinka. No other witnesses who were not victims of the Nazi regime, like for instance the camp guard Otto Horn, testified in the courtroom. The other reason is that the Nazi crimes in Treblinka were of historical proportions; the subjective cost of setting free the murderer of 850,000 people might outweigh the cost of convicting one innocent man.

Belief in the presence of the criminal
The second influence on the location of the decision criterion is the belief that the picture of the perpetrator is actually in the spread. This influence was also demonstrated by the effects of biased and unbiased instructions, discussed before: when witnesses are not advised that the perpetrator may not be in the lineup, the decision criterion shifts to the left, so that false alarm rates above 80 percent become possible. Witnesses in the Demjanjuk case were not routinely warned that possibly none of the pictures represented one of their guards. On the contrary, as we will see later, the photospreads often suggested that they consisted of nothing but Nazi criminals. Moreover, four out of the five who testified in court had correctly identified Fedor Fedorenko, another guard from Treblinka, in the same photospread. This could have increased their confidence in the ability of the investigators to come up with the guilty people.

Risk of being caught
The third influence on the adoption of a decision criterion
is the risk of being caught in a false declaration. A normal
lineup consists of one suspect and a number of known innocent foils. With a criterion which is too lenient, witnesses
may erroneously identify not only an innocent suspect, but
also a foil. In the latter case witnesses would reveal themselves as unreliable, thus undermining every detail of their
further testimony. The fear of doing this, especially when
much value is attached to the conviction of the suspect,
should prevent witnesses from adopting a decision criterion
which is too lenient. In a lineup of one, witnesses run no
risk of being caught out, and this is why one-person confrontations should be considered unreliable in cases of disputed
identity. In the Demjanjuk case there was another reason
why the risk of being caught out was small, or was gauged
to be small. This reason was that all people in the lineup
were suspected of Nazi crimes. Demjanjuk was first
suspected of being a guard in the death camp Sobibor.
When Eugen Turowski and Abraham Goldfarb, the first
Treblinka survivors who identified Demjanjuk as Ivan,
made their identification, this response could have been
classified as an error. But the opposite happened. The
charge against Demjanjuk was adapted to the identification,
which could be done because he was not an innocent foil.
The witnesses could have been aware of the fact that a
positive response would always lead to a prosecution, and
that therefore the risk of being caught making a false identification was zero.

Strong belief in memory
The decision criterion is also affected by a strong belief that
victims will always remember their torturers. Many victims
declare in the courtroom that they see the face of the
criminal in their dreams, and that they will never forget this
face. After making such a statement it will be difficult for
a witness to be hesitant in an identification test. The belief
that one will never forget is almost a commitment to a
clearcut response. In case of a doubtful recognition one may
tend to respond with more confidence than is warranted by

the actual resemblance. The witness Pinchas Epstein declared in the Jerusalem court:

> There are certain features which after so many years are marked in one's memory and cannot be erased. I see Ivan every night. My poor wife, I dream about Ivan every night. I envision him every night, he is imprinted in my memory. I cannot free myself of these impressions. (JET, 910)*

It is quite possible that Epstein is right, that he has a durable image of Ivan in his memory, and that therefore his identification was correct. But such statements can also mean that witnesses deny the possibility of a mistake, and that for this reason they have shifted their response criterion to the left.

Knowledge of previous successes
The fifth influence on the location of the decision criterion is the knowledge that other witnesses made a positive identification before, since this provides another reason for believing that the perpetrator is in the lineup. The underlying assumption of the presentation of a lineup to more than one witness is that these witnesses provide independent testimony. Ideally witnesses should not be allowed to speak to each other before their testimony is completed. This is the reason why future witnesses are not allowed to sit in the courtroom when other witnesses testify. Dependence among witnesses can originate in many different ways. One way is that witnesses talk to each other. This may happen even though two witnesses are heard on different days; they may happen to be family or close friends. Another way is through the news media. When newspapers publish the contents of a testimony in court, and this testimony contains a positive identification, it is reasonable for future witnesses to assume that the criminal is in the lineup. A very clear case is the investigation of Marinus De Rijke (Chapter 1), where the identification was not only announced but was also shown

---

* Throughout the book quotations from the Jerusalem trial will be referred to as JET (standing for Jerusalem English Transcript), and a page number. Quotations from the written statements produced by the police investigators are not referenced, as they were only submitted as evidence, without being a part of the trial transcript. These documents are listed by exhibit numbers in the bibliography.

on television. The same sort of involvement of the media can be expected when a trial is repeated after a number of years, following an appeal, or in a different country. A third avenue for information among witnesses runs via the investigators. Most written testimonies start with a simple statement in which the investigator explains the nature of the interview. Usually this means that the investigator mentions the name of the wanted criminal, but the sentence might conceal a much longer explanation of what happened before. Then follows an interview, in which the identification parade takes place, but the report about this interview contains only the answers to questions, not the questions themselves. Often such interviews last one hour or more, which provides ample opportunity for the communication of information about previous testimonies. A final way of telling the witnesses that previous witnesses were successful is by communicating that the investigations started a long time ago. A witness might easily come to the conclusion that the investigations against a suspect would have come to a halt, unless there were positive identifications by previous witnesses. The thickness of the investigator's file, for instance, would be a sufficient signal. Many of these elements were present in the Demjanjuk case, as we will see in later chapters. The witnesses knew each other very well in most instances, and it is unlikely that they did not meet between the interviews.

The shifting of decision criteria is amply studied in laboratory conditions, but the specific aspects of a forensic setting have rarely been the topic of extensive research. One exception is the influence of instructions to witnesses, mentioned above (pp. 42–43). This influence appeared to be extremely powerful: the percentage of positive responses in target-absent lineups was 33 percent when the instruction stressed that the target might not be in the lineup, and 78 percent when it did not. There is ample reason to believe that other influences may cause similar shifts of the decision criterion, but as it stands now, the assumption that all influences listed in this section will have effects rests more on common sense and logic than on experimental proof.

SPECIFIC BIAS IN UNFAIR LINEUPS

In the previous paragraphs I have demonstrated that the false identification of a suspect in a target-absent lineup is enhanced by the tendency towards making positive responses. But, as explained in Chapter 1, there is a second line of defense. Even when witnesses respond to target-absent lineups, there is no special reason why they should point to the suspect instead of a foil. If they don't, their response will immediately be recognized as incorrect. But it is also possible that the lineup is composed such that witnesses, once they make a positive identification, will automatically focus on the suspect. Reasons for this focussing may be that the suspect is in some dimensions clearly distinguishable from the foils, or that the suspect is the only participant that fits the general description of the perpetrator. Following a proposal by Doob and Kirshenbaum (1973) it is generally accepted that a way of measuring the unfair direction of attention to the suspect can be achieved using the assistance of subjects who had never been confronted with the suspect. Usually these subjects receive a general description of the crime and the criminal. Then they are confronted with the lineup, and asked to select the person who is most likely to be the target. When the suspect attracts an excess of votes, the lineup is said to be unfair. Various statistical measures of unfairness were proposed by Malpass (1981). Our main question is: which factors cause specific bias for selection of the suspect in a lineup? Six such factors will be discussed.

Resemblance between suspect and foils
The first and most obvious factor is the resemblance between the suspect and the foils, or the degree to which the foils fit the general description of the perpetrator. This relates to what Malpass (1981) calls the effective size of a lineup, as opposed to the nominal size. The simple idea is that implausible foils contribute less, or not at all, to the effective size of a lineup. I, myself, have testified about a lineup of six, including three foils with moustaches. The witnesses had stated that the robber was 'cleanshaven';

hence the effective size was reduced to no more than three (Krijger v. O.M., 1988). In another case my testimony was about the identification of a murderer who was described as small, between 30 and 40 years old, with long blond curls. The suspect was 1.70 meters tall, 38 years old, and with long blond curls. One of the foils was 1.91 meters tall, another was 62 years old, the third had a black beard, the fourth was a man of Indonesian descent with short, straight, pitchblack hair. The effective size of this lineup was therefore reduced to one (Britting v. O.M., 1988).

From the theoretical and professional literature it is not at all clear how foils are to be selected. One obvious rule is that all foils should fit a general description, which is obtained from the witnesses prior to the construction of the identity parade. These descriptions should not only refer to gender, race, age, hair color and style, beard and moustache, body height and weight, general form of the face, but also to highly specific features.

Malpass and Devine (1983) studied mock lineup trials in which the wanted person was described as having brown, medium-long wavy hair, of medium size and build, and with dark eyes. The suspect always fitted this description, while the number of differences between suspect and foils were varied systematically up to about five.

The tendency of mock witnesses to select the suspect varied accordingly from 10 to 80 percent. A consequence of this finding is that it is impossible to confront witnesses with a lineup when their initial description does not match the suspect. The reason is that selection according to all the witnesses' descriptions would lead to foils that look different from the suspect.

A special problem is created by the effect of distinctive versus typical faces. It may be remembered that a target with a distinctive face elicits more hits and fewer false alarms. The reverse might happen when a foil has a distinctive face. Take the extreme case of a well-known public personality serving as a foil in a lineup because he fits the general description of gender, age, race, size, etc. A witness would never be misled by this foil, and the presence of such a foil would decrease the effective size of the lineup. The same will happen when the face of the foil is not well known, but very distinctive. Witnesses will immediately realize that the man with the big scar is not the one they saw before. Such a foil also does not contribute to the effective size of the lineup. Unfortunately there is no way in which the distinctiveness of the foils can be assessed on an *a priori* basis. Only the actual test with a reasonable number of mock witnesses can establish whether and to what extent foils contribute to the effective size, but in many cases an extensive test of fairness will be highly impracticable.

Outstanding features
Witnesses tend to focus upon the suspect when for one or another reason the suspect is markedly different from the foils. The difference could be in facial marks like a scar or a beard, in the clothing, in the posture, or anything. I have dealt with a lineup containing five policemen with black shoes, and one suspect in sneakers. The participants were marked by numbers, and these numbers were placed between their feet, so that the witnesses could not fail to notice the sneakers (Krijger v. O.M., 1988).

In a photographic lineup the difference could be in such aspects as the size of the picture or the size of the face in the picture; one unofficial picture among police mugshots, one vague picture among clear ones, and so on. A clear case is the investigation against Willy Darden, convicted in 1974 for murder in the State of Florida, and executed in 1988 (Darden v. Wainwright, 1983 and Darden v. Wainwright, 1986). Willy Darden's picture was the only one with a name and a date on it among a number of unmarked foils. In a study by Buckhout (1974) it was demonstrated that the one picture that is different is more likely to be selected as the criminal's portrait.

In a case study with 100 mock witnesses I asked students to select from a six-person lineup the one person who was most likely to be the criminal, and to give their reasons. It appeared that 54 percent looked at the expression or posture adopted by the participants (tries to look innocent, does not know where to look, looks worried). These results indicate that participants in a lineup should get clear instructions on how to look, and how to stand.

Number of foils
When the number of foils is too small, there may be a considerable danger that witnesses who have no reliable memories will identify the suspect just by chance. The probability of accidental identification by witnesses who base their response on guessing is simply the inverse of the number of participants. It was argued by Malpass (1981) that for this computation of guessing level, one should not take the nominal size of the lineup, but the effective size, which is based on the number of foils that appear to be plausible choice alternatives in a test employing mock witnesses. Usually effective size is considerably smaller than nominal size. However, it should be realized that there is a difference between mock witnesses and real witnesses. Mock witnesses are encouraged to guess, which is the reason why probability of guessing is an appropriate measure of the fairness of a test. But instructions to real witnesses usually discourage guessing, and the effect is that the probability of accidental identification of the suspect is in reality much lower. This is easily seen when the lineup consists of one person, the suspect. Real witnesses do not always identify the suspect in a one-person lineup (also called a showup) because they do not always recognize the suspect. Lineup size has little effect when guessing can be kept at a minimum. The guessing level of mock witnesses can therefore only be used as an estimate of the upper risk margin. I have encountered a case of a lineup of only three and two witnesses, of whom only one made a correct identification. The probability of such a result in the case of pure guessing, computed according to the binomial formula is $p=0.44$. This does not mean that the witnesses *were* guessing, but the probative value of the test was low, since the result was not unlikely, even when the witnesses were guessing.

The literature does not contain useful suggestions for the choice of lineup size. From the tables presented by Malpass (1981) one could infer that a lineup of five to ten people is acceptable, but this range is not supported by any reasonable argument.

As reported before, the number of false alarms in lineups is smaller when the lineup gets bigger, probably because the *embarras du choix* makes witnesses aware of their incomplete knowledge. In a small lineup it is possible that only one participant looks like the wanted criminal. In larger lineups it is more likely to have two or more plausible candidates, and the choice dilemma may prevent positive responses.

A suggestion encountered frequently is that small lineups can be made more reliable by employing more witnesses. This is, in principle, true when witnesses are mutually independent and guessing, because the probability that successive witnesses all make the correct guess by accident becomes smaller and smaller. But when witnesses make mistakes, not because they are guessing, but because the lineup is unfair, or because the suspect bears an unfortunate resemblance to the perpetrator, there is a high probability that all witnesses will be misled in the same way. The computed guessing level can be very small in a case with multiple witnesses, but this does not mean that a high identification rate is a reliable result. The impact of multiple witnesses is large when the alternative to correct recognition is guessing. It may well be zero when the alternative explanation is an unfair lineup procedure or a close resemblance. When multiple witnesses concur for an artifactual reason, the impact will be negative, if the concurrence inspires the court or the jury with an unwarranted confidence. The problem of multiple witnesses played an important role in the Demjanjuk case, as we will see in Chapters 4 and 5.

Guilty appearance
Some witnesses believe that villains in general can be recognized by their faces. The result is that a suspect who fits the stereotypical image of a villain will be more likely to be identified by witnesses. An illustration was provided by the previously mentioned lineup test employing 100 mock witnesses, conducted in my laboratory. The choice rates for the six participants were: 32, 19, 19, 13, 10, and 7 percent. The reason for choosing the most preferred participant was

in 47 percent of the cases the guilty expression on his face. Again it should be stressed that the guilty appearance of the suspect is a disturbing factor only when witnesses are partly guessing.

Repeated exposure
When witnesses are, in the course of investigative procedures, confronted with the suspect or a picture of the suspect, they may identify the same person in a subsequent lineup for that reason alone. The explanation is that a face may look familiar even when one does not know where or when it was seen before. The inference that familiarity must be due to the fact that this face belongs to the criminal is called 'unconscious transference'. Loftus (1979) mentions the example of a train clerk who sold tickets to a sailor in a railway station. Later the clerk identified the sailor in a lineup as the perpetrator of a criminal act he had witnessed, ostensibly because the suspect looked familiar to him. Effects of unconscious transference have been reported in a number of experimental studies. Typical situations in which it may occur are the presentation of mugshots prior to an identity parade, or the conduct of successive identity parades. The witness Anna Kremski in the investigation of Frank Walus (see Chapter 1) was presented with one set of pictures in a hotel lobby in Tel Aviv, and probably with another set at the Immigration Service in New York. It is not certain but quite probable that only Frank Walus's picture appeared in both sets. Under such conditions unconscious transference is a real danger. We will see that most witnesses in the Demjanjuk case were exposed to two photospreads that had only a representation of Demjanjuk in common.

Unconscious suggestion
There is an extensive literature demonstrating that interviewers unintentionally transmit information to their subjects. The classical text on this topic by Rosenthal (1966) illustrates that these experimenter effects are ubiquitous and almost impossible to suppress as long as the interviewers know the desired answer. A famous example is the case of 'Kluge Hans' (Clever Hans) a horse that was claimed to

perform complicated calculations (Pfungst, 1911). Hans responded by stamping on the ground the correct number of times. Of course it appeared after a while that the trainer, who knew the correct answer, made an unconscious and minute gesture when the correct number was reached, and that Hans had grown very sensitive to this gesture.

In the same way it is possible that police investigators communicate their knowledge to witnesses when they inspect a lineup. The remedy against such unconscious transmissions is the adoption of a double blind procedure, which means that neither the investigators nor the witnesses know who the suspect is. This situation is in reality never encountered. A lesser protection is obtained when the actual confrontation is being videotaped, or recorded on a tape recorder, so that at least a posterior check can be made. Even this is rarely done in practice. In the case of Demjanjuk there were not even verbatim transcripts made of what was said to the witnesses prior to, and during the confrontations. It is also unclear how much time the witnesses needed to respond, although in one case a period of over half an hour is mentioned. It is almost impossible for an investigator not to exert any influence during such a long period of doubt, pondering and deliberation.

The opportunity of influencing the witness may depend upon the way in which the identity parade is conducted. A properly timed live lineup seen through a one-way mirror could be safer than a stack of pictures manipulated by the investigator. But even with a live lineup it is often up to the investigator to accept a response and stop, or to continue the session until the desired response is obtained. The investigator might be completely honest when doing this, reasoning, for instance, that the mistaken witness was not 100 percent certain and should therefore be allowed more time.

A strong form of suggestion is specifically asking questions about one participant, or one picture, such as 'Don't you recognize number five?' The result of such a direct question is that the effective lineup size is immediately reduced to one. As said before, such errors will rarely become evident, because confrontations are not recorded on tape or in verbatim protocols, while errors will tend to be omitted from later statements. But we will see that similar direct suggestive questions were asked and reported by the Demjanjuk investigators.

CONFIDENCE

There is a general tendency to attach more weight to identifications when witnesses express great confidence. Usually investigators report whether a witness seemed to be confident, and the intention of such a report is obviously to add weight to the evidence. This intuition was given a legal status by the United States Supreme Court's ruling in *Neil v. Biggers* (1972), where confidence of the witness was specified as a criterion for the assessment of the accuracy of an identification procedure. However, it is firmly established that confidence and identification accuracy are not closely related. A number of studies have reported small correlations, zero correlations, and even negative correlations between confidence and accuracy. Deffenbacher (1980) predicted that a loss of correlation can be counteracted by variables that promote correct encoding, but this prediction was proved to be wrong by Cutler *et al.* (1987). Deffenbacher (1988) referred to a meta-analysis of 40 confidence-accuracy studies; the average correlation was $r=0.25$. This number illustrates clearly that in general witnesses are poor judges of the reliability of their statements. The process leading to an incorrect identification can, at the same time, generate the cues that prompt high levels of confidence. I have shown (Wagenaar, 1988a) that confidence and accuracy are most likely to be uncorrelated when people base their recollections on logical reconstruction instead of direct retrieval from memory. High levels of confidence reflect the plausibility of the reconstruction, but not necessarily the truth, because life is not always plausible. One witness in the case of Marinus De Rijke exchanged the identities of the victim and his assailant. The witness remembered the event and one name. Is it not a plausible reconstruction that this name belongs to the camp guard, whom he remembered so well, and not to the victim who was hardly known to him?

The relevant question, then, is whether witnesses have reasons and means to rely on logical reconstruction when direct retrieval from memory is not successful. Reasons were already listed in the section on target-absent lineups. In reality the means problem hardly occurs because witnesses are not asked to sketch a portrait from memory; they are only requested to look at and point to one of the people in the lineup. When the memory of the original event does not contain a clear image of the criminal's face, one does not need any special means for substituting a face of someone in that lineup. The result is a memory of the event, with a clear representation of the criminal, which coincides nicely with one of the people in the lineup. The substitution of later stimuli in earlier memories is very much like the effects of misleading post-event information first described by Elizabeth Loftus and her co-workers (cf. Loftus, 1979; Loftus, Miller and Burns, 1978; Wagenaar and Boer, 1987). Especially the study on the effects of presenting misleading post-event information with respect to faces (Loftus and Greene, 1980) makes this point very clear. Post-event information can originate reconstructions of faces seen before, to such an extent that a beardless person gets a beard, or a luxuriant hairdo is recalled as baldness.

Once the substitution has been made, it will lead to increasing confidence at each subsequent confrontation with the suspect because the suspect's face appears to resemble the remembered face over and over again. Especially when the time between the first identity parade and later confrontations is extensive, it will be increasingly difficult for a witness to realize that the familiarity stems from the lineup session, not from the crime.

The time needed for the first recognition of a suspect in an identity parade could give a clue with respect to what is going on inside the witness: immediate recognition or slow reconstruction. Unfortunately recognition times are hardly ever recorded. The recognition of Demjanjuk's picture was not always immediate. On the contrary, some subjects

needed a long time, which provided them sufficient oppor-
tunities to reconstruct their memories unconsciously. At the
same time quite a few of the witnesses expressed less than
100 percent confidence. Five witnesses made identifications
in the courtroom with great confidence *ten* years after their
first identifications. It cannot be expected that witnesses
would be able to distinguish between their original
memories and the reconstructions thereof, made ten years
ago.

CONCLUSION

This short review of some relevant literature has shown
that identification of people by eyewitnesses is not always
reliable, and that the reliability depends upon a multitude
of aspects. Cutler *et al.* (1987) called these aspects estimator
variables and system variables. Estimator variables are those
variables that are not under the control of the investigating
authority; examples are the exposure time during the crime
and the degree of violence. System variables are those that
are related to the investigative procedure, and that are
therefore under the control of the investigators; examples
in the context of identification tests are instructions to the
witnesses and fairness of the lineup. Estimator variables can
be used only to make an assessment of the reliability of the
witnesses' memories. In the case of Demjanjuk I have
argued that little is known about the effect of estimator
variables, when it comes to the memories of death camp
survivors. The study by Wagenaar and Groeneweg (1988)
is only a first attempt to fill the gap.

In the remaining chapters only a little will be said about
the estimator variables that may have affected the memories
of the witnesses in the Demjanjuk case. With regard to
system variables the situation is different. One can always
request that an identification procedure, as part of the
factfinding process, is conducted in the best possible way,
and such that the result is minimally affected by system
variables. The fact that the charge involves the murder of
850,000 innocent people does not justify a reduction of

the standard of meticulousness that in other circumstances would be accepted as a normal requirement. For that reason the next chapter will be devoted to procedural rules for identity parades that can be inferred from studies on the effects of system variables.

3 Rules for the Conduct and Interpretation of Identity Tests

The literature reviewed in the previous chapter suggests a number of rules for the proper conduct and interpretation of identity tests. In a few countries some of these rules have been embodied in the legislation. A laudable and quite comprehensive discussion of rules was prepared by a British advisory committee chaired by Lord Devlin (1976). I will refer to this discussion as 'The Devlin Report'. In the following pages I will present a list of 50 practical rules for the conduct of identity parades and the interpretation of the outcomes that may help to protect police investigators and legal courts against a number of errors. Not all of these rules are sufficiently based upon available research, because a substantial amount of research has still to be done. But in uncertain cases, adoption of a conservative rule is dictated by the principle that a suspect should not be exposed to unnecessary risks. One can always define conservative rules on the basis of experience, reasonable assumptions, and logic.

LINEUP VERSUS SHOWUP

There are two different procedures which I will call lineup and showup. A lineup procedure employs an arrangement of one suspect and a number of innocent foils, while a showup confronts the witness with the suspect only. The aims of these two procedures are totally different.

A showup is used when the witness knows the suspect

very well for other reasons than involvement in the crime. A lineup would be useless in such a case, because the witness would always recognize the familiar person among a set of unfamiliar foils. The aim of a showup is only to ascertain that the police arrested the person indicated by the witness. The showup does not prove the relation between the suspect and the crime any more than the prior testimony about the suspect.

One example from my own experience is the identification of a masked man who robbed a jewelry store. The store owners claimed to have recognized the robber as a young man who visited the shop frequently, and who lived around the corner. The purpose of the showup was to make sure that the accused was indeed the boy whom they knew so well, not to prove that the shopowners were right when they said they had recognized the masked robber (Krenten v. O.M., 1986).

Another example from my own experience is a case of arson in the old tourist town of Volendam. Two women, mother and daughter, both working in the same bar, declared that they saw the arsonist when he ran away in the night. They recognized him, from the way he walked, as a regular visitor to their bar. The showup was only to ascertain that the police arrested the right client. Whether or not the two women correctly recognized the arsonist is a different question, which cannot be answered by means of a showup or a lineup (Wijmenga v. O.M., 1988).

A showup with a suspect known to the witness is not a test of perception or memory, but a verification of investigative procedure. Therefore a showup can never serve as a proof of identity when there is doubt about the perception or the memory of a witness. This conclusion was also reached by the Devlin Committee. They stated that 'A witness who claims to have had a fleeting glimpse of a close relative may, of course, be mistaken, but it is not a claim that could be tested by a parade' (p. 99). The Committee provided a number of examples of mistaken showup identifications:

A witness to a smash and grab raid identified one of the offenders as a man known to him by his nickname for about five years, and claimed to have confirmed this recognition when he got a half view of the man's face in the course of the chase that followed. The accused was acquitted at a re-trial when further alibi evidence was called.

A garage attendant who was the victim of an assault said that just before the attack, he thought he saw X whom he knew well by sight, standing at a nearby bus shelter. He subsequently positively identified X as his assailant, saying 'When he came towards me I recognized him as X himself . . . whilst I was being attacked I saw the face of the person attacking me. I recognized that face. It was Mr. X.' X was granted a Free Pardon when another was found reliably to have confessed to the offence.

A police witness to a daylight burglary claimed to recognize one of the participants two days later as a man known to him for some years by name and sight. It subsequently transpired that the witness had known the accused only by sight. He was granted a Free Pardon when another was found reliably to have confessed to the offence.

One of the officers who stopped a lorry which contained stolen butter said that as the lorry approached he had recognized the accused as the driver, but subsequent inquiries revealed he had not seen the man he identified before the time of the offence. The conviction was quashed when further evidence substantiated the accused's alibi. (pp. 70–71)

Taken together, the argument against showups is that identification of a person known to the witness does not prove involvement in the crime, and that showups have in the past produced mistaken identifications. This evidence, then, suggests the following rule:

RULE 1. **Involvement in a crime cannot be proved by means of a lineup or showup when the suspect is known to the witness for other reasons than involvement in the crime.**

A lineup is used for the identification of a suspect who is known to the witness only through his presence at the scene of the crime. In that case recognition can only be the result of the suspect's involvement in the crime, which means that recognition provides evidence of this involvement.

The diagnostic value of a lineup increases with the size of the lineup. A lineup of one has almost no diagnostic value and should be rejected if a larger lineup could have been put together. Therefore it will, in general, not be possible to use a showup in place of a lineup as a proof of identity. A good example of confusing showup and lineup is a case of kidnaping in which I testified. The kidnapper kept his victim imprisoned for a whole week. In that week there were many hours of contact. The suspect, who was arrested half a year later, denied any involvement in the crime. Perhaps the police were misled by the long confrontation period, which should have made the recognition in a lineup easy: instead they tried to prove their case by means of a showup. The kidnaper was known to the victim only through the crime, and therefore a properly conducted lineup could have yielded convincing evidence. As a result the case was lost, simply because the showup was rejected as unsafe. (Bumber v. O.M., 1985).

RULE 2. **Identification of a suspect not known to the witness for other reasons than the encounter during the crime should be achieved by means of a lineup, not a showup.**

TRACING VERSUS IDENTIFICATION

The tracing of an unknown suspect is not the same as the identification after a suspect has been apprehended. It is quite normal to confront the victim of a crime with an album of photographs representing people who committed similar crimes before. I will call this tracing procedure the inspection of mugfiles. The result of mugfile inspection is that the names of possible suspects are brought to the attention of the police, nothing more. The selection of a suspect through mugfile inspection does not constitute any proof against that suspect, because a mugfile does not conform to the requirements stated for identity parades and photographic lineups. One difference is the fact that a witness pointing to the wrong person in a mugfile is not easily caught making an error, because all people in the mugfile are possible suspects. There is also nothing amiss when the witness selects more than one picture from a mugfile. The purpose of mugfile inspection is to limit the number of suspects, not to construct evidence against a specific suspect.

Identification of a suspect through pictures taken from a mugfile is not as a matter of principle excluded. But it requires that the other pictures represent innocent foils, matched with the description of the suspect on a number of dimensions. There are more differences between the inspection of mugfiles and the identification of suspects but the foregoing is already sufficient for the formulation of the following rule.

RULE 3. **Selection of a suspect through mugfile inspection should not be used as a proof of identity.**

The tracing of suspects by means of mugfile inspection creates special risks that should be considered carefully. One is that mugfile inspection is limited to suspects already known to the police. Another risk, more relevant to the problem of subsequent identification, is that the witness who made the selection has now two competing memories: one of the criminal during the actual crime and one of the suspect on the selected picture. The two memories may form a blend, or worse, the later memory may replace the earlier one. In both cases it is obvious that a witness who assisted in the tracing of a suspect through mugfile inspection is more likely to identify that suspect in a subsequent identification test. Therefore I state the following rule.

RULE 4. **Witnesses who took part in a mugfile inspection should be excluded from later identification tests**.

Rule 4 creates problems when there are only few witnesses to a crime. Obviously there could be a conflict between initial tracing and subsequent identification, and the consequence of the rule should not be that perpetrators of crimes with few witnesses are no longer brought to trial. But, on the other hand, it is also not desirable to put suspects at extra risks, only because there are few witnesses. It is advisable to avoid mugfile confrontations in cases with few witnesses as long as possible. One solution to this problem could be the use of identikit reconstructions, or of portraits drawn after descriptions given by the witnesses, instead of mugfiles. This does not solve the problem entirely, but at least the risk is somewhat reduced.

In all cases, but especially when there is scarcity of witnesses, mugfile inspections should be stopped as soon as the name of a suspect who can be placed in an identity parade is known. The same applies when the picture of that suspect can be arranged in a properly composed photo-spread. This leads to the following rule.

RULE 5. Witnesses should not be used for mugfile inspection when a proper identification test can be conducted.

A third disadvantage of tracing suspects through mugfile inspection is that it will, almost by definition, produce suspects who look like the wanted criminal. Compare this to another search method, for instance the selection of the three people who had access to a building in a burglary case. A subsequent identity parade would bring totally new evidence, because the suspects were not selected on the basis of their resemblance to the criminal. It would be quite informative should one of the three people with access to the building also happen to resemble the criminal. With selection on the basis of mugfile inspection the case is different. All suspects selected this way can be expected to resemble the criminal. A subsequent identity parade therefore creates a greater risk of a false positive. A selection made in a mugfile inspection, under conditions not accepted as proper for an identity parade, might erroneously produce candidates who can no longer be protected by the controls of a properly conducted identity parade. Therefore an identity parade preceded by mugfile inspection should carry less weight.

RULE 6. An identification test preceded by a mugfile inspection should carry less weight, even when different witnesses are employed.

From the foregoing it is clear that mugfile inspection should be restricted to a minimum. The same conclusion was reached in the Devlin Report:

Once the police have got a suspect whom they can put on parade, further steps towards identification should be taken by means of the parade and not by the showing of photographs. We do not propose that this should be an absolute rule since the needs of the investigation must be paramount, but we consider that any departure from it should call for justification. We recommend a statutory provision that a witness who has been shown a photograph of the accused shall not be permitted to make an identification in court unless the judge, having regard to the Rules, is satisfied that the showing was reasonably necessary for the purposes of the investigation. (p. 151)

REPEATED TESTING

The use of the same witnesses both for mugfile inspection and identification is an example of repeated testing. The general problem of repeated testing is that witnesses may remember the previous tests, and that these memories may operate as misleading post-event information. Examples from my own experience are the following cases.

A suspect was selected from a mugfile by the only witness to a crime. The suspect was arrested half a year later, when he tried to enter the country through Amsterdam Airport. A showup was held, in which the witness was confronted with the suspect sitting in his cell. The witness said this person looked familiar to him. The question is of course why? Did he remember him from the scene of the crime, or from seeing his picture at the police station? (Bumber v. O.M., 1985).

Another suspect was identified in a lineup procedure by two tellers of the bank that the suspect had allegedly robbed. In order to make sure that the witnesses were not mistaken, a second attempt was made with the same parade, but with the participants in a different order. The witness pointed to the same man. Why? Because he recognized him again, or because he remembered to which person he had pointed five minutes ago? (Krijger v. O.M., 1988).

In a similar situation another investigator decided to repeat the test with the same suspect, but different foils. The witness pointed to the same man, but that was of course the only man he had seen in the other lineup (Poelstra v. O.M., 1988).

Investigators should in principle follow the next rule strictly, and if this is not possible a full explanation should be provided.

RULE 7. No witness should be asked to identify the same suspect more than once.

A special situation is the repetition of an identification test in court. Usually this concerns single confrontations rather than identity parades, but photospreads have also been shown to witnesses in court for the second time. Sometimes these repeated identifications are required by protocol, and therefore cannot be avoided. But witnesses can be much more certain the second time because of the effects of post-event information. It would be completely wrong if a court or a jury accepted this degree of certainty as indicative of the certainty with which the identification was made originally.

More about this will be said in the section on dock identifications. At present it will suffice to state that identifications repeated in the courtroom should have no evidential value whatsoever, simply because of Rule 7. For the same reason there should be absolute certainty that there were no previous unrecorded identification attempts, such as the one by Anna Kremski in the case of Frank Walus.

THE PROBATIVE VALUE OF AN IDENTIFICATION

An identification test is required when otherwise there would be some degree of uncertainty with respect to the identity of the perpetrator. The final court decision depends on two independent quantities: the degree of uncertainty that exists without the results of the identification test, and the probative value of the test. In a way one could say that the prosecution presents the results of an identification test in order to turn an initial uncertainty into a certainty beyond reasonable doubt. Whether or not an identification test will achieve this objective depends to a large extent upon the probative value of the test.

The probative value of an identification test is determined by its diagnosticity of guilt or innocence. When the guilty are always identified, and the innocent are not, the test is perfectly diagnostic. On the other hand, when many guilty people are not recognized in a lineup, while innocent suspects are mistaken for criminals, diagnosticity is limited. A quantitative expression of diagnosticity is provided by the ratio of the likelihoods of identifying guilty and innocent people. Without entering elaborate and rather complicated mathematical analyses, it can be stated that, according to the empirical literature, diagnosticity of identification tests is generally low. This implies that in cases of total initial uncertainty about the identity of the criminal, the probative value of an identity test will not suffice to remove all doubt. Or, in other words, there should be reasons to suspect the accused, besides the identifications by eyewitnesses. The problem is somewhat lessened by the employment of large effective lineup sizes because diagnosticity can be shown to increase linearly with lineup size.

From this discussion it is clear that there are two conditions for the use of identification tests. One is a sufficient effective size, which I will discuss later. The other is a reason to assume a substantial prior probability of guilt. Without further evidence there is no reason to conclude that a person is guilty only because he was identified in a lineup. In actual court cases it is customary to start the trial with the assumption that the accused is not guilty, which means that the prior odds of guilt are very low. If there is no other evidence than identification by an eyewitness, the odds will remain too low to convict.

This view is supported by the Devlin Report:

The possibility of mistake in visual identification is sufficiently high to mean that as a rule evidence of visual identification standing by itself should not be allowed to raise the level of probability of guilt up to the standard of reasonable certainty that is required by the criminal law. (p. 86)

And later:

We are satisfied that in cases which depend wholly or mainly on eyewitness evidence of identification there is a special risk of wrong conviction. It arises because the value of such evidence is exceptionally difficult to assess; the witness who has sincerely convinced himself and whose sincerity carries conviction is not infrequently mistaken. . . The only way of diminishing the risk is by increasing the burden of proof. . . We do however wish to ensure that in ordinary cases prosecutions are not brought on eyewitness evidence only and that, if brought, they will fail. We think that they ought to fail, since in our opinion it is only in exceptional cases that identification evidence is by itself sufficiently reliable to exclude a reasonable doubt about guilt. (pp. 149–50)

In accord with this the following rule is suggested.

RULE 8. **Identification by an eyewitness should not be accepted as evidence, if there is no further evidence of guilt.**

In the next section I will discuss what this further evidence should consist of.

MULTIPLE WITNESSES

A complicated question concerns the probative value of identifications by different witnesses. This question was raised by Judge Tal in the Jerusalem court when he asked whether the probability of the same mistake being made by several witnesses can be computed by multiplying the probabilities that single witnesses each would make that mistake. The answer is in principle negative. Before discussing the joint probability of all witnesses making the same mistake, I will first enter a related issue: can the corrobative evidence, mentioned in Rule 8, consist of identification by another witness? The Devlin Report came to the following conclusion:

In a number of the leading cases of misidentification there has been corroboration in the shape of direct testimony from a second witness. In Beck's case 15 women, whom it was alleged that he had defrauded, independently identified him. In Slater's case there were over a dozen (but there was no proper identification parade) and in Warner's case there were 17.

This suggests that the testimony of a second eye-witness does not offer much additional protection. Such a suggestion is strongly reinforced by the two cases of Dougherty and Virag. Even where police officers work in pairs or more, they make independent identifications on the parade. But there seems to be a tendency for them, when there is a mistake, to make the same mistake. The tendency is not confined to policemen; it exists whenever two witnesses are involved in the same incident, as in the case of Dougherty. (pp. 77–78)

And further on:

In paragraphs 4.29–32 above, we considered whether or not a second witness should be regarded as corroboration. The danger to be guarded against, however, is not the untruthfulness or unreliability of a single individual (in which case evidence to the same effect from another individual would be strengthening) but the unreliability of eye-witness evidence in general. Therefore, we accept the argument of *Justice* that the additional supporting evidence should be evidence of a different kind, i.e. evidence other than of visual identification. (p. 89)

In addition the Devlin Committee reached the conclusion that identification of a criminal not known to the witness is unreliable, even when there has been a prolonged confrontation in the context of the crime. 'It would certainly be necessary to tell the jury that even under such circumstances mistakes have been made' (p. 89). It was already stated in Rule 1 that involvement in the crime cannot be proved by means of a lineup or showup when witnesses knew the suspect before. Together these two conclusions mean that even after frequent or prolonged observation, identification by eyewitnesses cannot by itself prove involvement in the crime.

The rejection of other identifications as corroborating evidence is logically founded upon the distinction between *analytical* and *synthetic* proof. Analytical proof of guilt is the result of a process of deductive reasoning, through which the number of suspects is limited from many to few. If it can be shown that only one person had the opportunity to kill the victim, that would be an example of analytical proof of guilt. The Trawniki document, if genuine, is an example of analytical proof that Demjanjuk was trained as a Nazi camp guard. Analytical proof reasons from facts to the suspect. Synthetic proof of guilt works in the opposite direction. One starts with a suspect and checks whether he fits the facts. If the criminal is known to be a fast runner, then that fact would help little to trace a suspect, because there are too many fast runners in the world. But if there is a suspect, one can check whether he is a fast runner. If he is, that would constitute synthetic proof of the suspect's guilt. The problem of synthetic proof is that we can never be certain of having excluded all other suspects. If our suspect is a fast runner, there are many others who fit this description equally well. Even if the suspect is the only one who fits the description, usually we only know that by checking all other people in the world.

Identification by eyewitnesses is a form of synthetic proof of guilt. It can be attempted, once there is a suspect, but it will never yield a suspect when there is none. An identification test may reveal that a suspect resembles the criminal sufficiently for the witness to see no difference. But there could be many people in the world who meet this criterion equally well, or even better. We can only exclude this possibility by inspecting all other people. Further tests, by other witnesses but with the same suspect, will be of no avail. The only reason why the real perpetrator is different from all other suspects who look like him is that there may be an analytical proof that connects the real perpetrator to the circumstances of the crime. More synthetic proof of guilt does not preclude mistaken identity; only analytical proof may do that. Therefore, besides controlling the quality of identification tests, it is necessary to ask 'Why this suspect? How did they get the idea of placing this person in a lineup?' If the answer is 'Because of other identifications', there is something wrong. The ideal procedure is to trace the suspect through an analytical process, and then to verify his identity through the synthetic process of an identity test. This is the purpose of Rule 9.

RULE 9. **Proof of identity through an identification test should be corroborated by supporting evidence of a different kind, not by other identification tests, even when they employ different witnesses.**

An example demonstrating the distinction between analytical and synthetic proof is provided by the problem of alibi. I will not discuss this issue at any great length, although the Devlin Committee devoted many pages to it. In principle the availability of a credible alibi is accepted as a negation of positive identifications. The problem is what should be done about a *missing* alibi. In the context of analytical versus synthetic proof the answer is obvious. The absence of alibi is synthetic proof; thousands of people will not be able to provide an alibi for that particular time.

Hence the absence of alibi can never constitute the evidence needed to corroborate positive identifications. Rule 9 leads immediately to the question: 'Why interrogate more than one witness?' The first reason was already presented above: witnesses could be deliberately lying. The second reason is more important. It is that, even when confirming evidence is not very informative, the same cannot be said of disconfirming evidence. The identification by one witness can be nullified by the failure of a subsequent witness. The investigators should not be set on verifying a preconceived conviction, but on falsifying a suspicion that could be wrong. The presentation of multiple positive identifications demonstrates that the investigators attempted falsification, but failed to disprove the accusation. A failure to question more witnesses when they were available suggests an unacceptable degree of carelessness on the part of the investigators.

RULE 10. When there are more witnesses available, falsification of an initial identification should be attempted.

Naturally the objective of falsification, or of the demonstration of failed falsification, can be achieved only when all identification tests are reported. Selective reporting of only positive identifications would create the impression that falsification was attempted but not achieved, and this impression would be wrong. Usually one is forced to rely on the honesty of the investigators because there is no way to check the completeness of their reporting. A solution to this problem is proposed by the Devlin Committee:

The prosecution should be required by statute to supply the defence on request with the name and addresses of any witness, whether or not he attends a parade, who is known to them as having seen the criminal in the circumstances of the crime, together with a copy of the description, if any, of the criminal given by such a person. (p. 151)

The observance of this rule would enable the defense to check whether identifications were attempted but left unreported. Another way to deal with this problem is by requiring that defense counsel is always present at identifications, be they live parades or photo identity tests. The Devlin Report comments on this solution:

> While it is desirable that a suspect should always have a solicitor representing him at a parade, this is not an indispensable requirement. If, however, the accused's solicitor is not present the officer investigating the case should be excluded from the parade. (p. 153)

Whatever the means are for assuring that all identification trials are reported, the rule is obvious.

RULE 11. **All identification attempts, whether successful or not, must be reported.**

When some of the witnesses do not identify the suspect in an identification test, the aggregate result should not be treated as the outcome of some sort of soccer match. A result of five positive identifications against two negative ones does not mean that the positives have won. Instead it is necessary to provide a sufficient account of why some witnesses failed to identify the suspect. It is possible that these witnesses had less opportunity to observe the criminal; that their initial description of the criminal was already vague or inaccurate; or that other aspects of their testimony were also demonstrably wrong. But a negative result produced by an otherwise reliable witness, who gave a detailed description of the criminal, poses a serious problem to the prosecution because it means that, according to the witness, the suspect is not the same person as the criminal. Therefore there should be a detailed discussion of negative results in the report of the identification tests.

Rule 12. **Reports about identification attempts with negative results should provide all available information that could help to understand the failure.**

It should be recognized that police investigators do not primarily involve more witnesses in order to obtain negative results. The objective is to strengthen the case through the collection of confirming evidence. We have already concluded that eyewitness identification can never constitute sufficient proof when identity is in dispute. The question is, whether identification by more witnesses can at least strengthen the case. A positive identification of the suspect is either the correct identification of the criminal, or the incorrect identification of an innocent person. The only reason why a full recognition of an innocent person could have occurred is that this person shared a sufficient number of features with the real criminal to cause a confusion. The question whether the suspect *is* the criminal or *looks very much* like the criminal cannot reliably be solved by the employment of further eyewitnesses, because, if the suspect does in fact look like the criminal, the next witnesses are bound to make the same mistake. Thus, while the non-identification by further witnesses provides significant information, we must not give too much weight to corroboration by further witnesses.

RULE 13. The probative value of an initial identification is only marginally increased through identification by other eyewitnesses.

Another problem introduced by the employment of multiple witnesses is the risk of contacts among witnesses during the hearings. This problem is relatively small when witnesses do not know each other, or when all witnesses can be heard immediately after the crime. But in some cases it will appear that witnesses have ties of family or close friendship so that they have had ample opportunity to talk to each other before or between the hearings.

This is not easily avoided, as witnesses are not always available immediately after the crime. One example, mentioned earlier in this chapter, is of a mother and daughter, who both observed an arsonist in Volendam, and who were questioned two and a half months after the event. One must assume that the two had discussed the case between them.

Contact among witnesses must be avoided as much as possible because they may provide each other with post-event information. They may tend to present this information, unconsciously or deliberately, as if it formed a part of their own observation.

RULE 14. Investigators should do everything within their power to prevent contacts among witnesses.

This point is also stressed in the Devlin Report:

Witnesses should . . . so far as is practicable having regard to the circumstances of the case, be prevented from talking with each other. (p. 153)

As I have said, it will not always be possible to prevent contacts among witnesses because they might have occurred even before the witnesses were known to the investigators. But at least it should be established whether or not witnesses had discussed aspects of the case with each other. Contacts with other people, who did not or will not serve as witnesses, could be equally detrimental because these others could also provide post-event information not previously known to the witnesses.

RULE 15. Investigators should ask witnesses, before the identification attempt, whether or not they discussed the case with other people. The answers to such questions should be carefully recorded.

If witnesses indicate that they received information from other people, be they witnesses or not, then excluding these witnesses from taking part in an identification test should be considered. If other witnesses are not easy to obtain, it will be necessary to determine how much information about the identity of the criminal was exchanged.

RULE 16. Witnesses should be excluded from an identification test if it is established that they could base their identification partly or wholly on information transmitted by other people.

PRIOR DESCRIPTION OF THE SUSPECT

Prior to the composition of an identity parade or photo-spread it will be necessary to obtain from the witnesses a verbal description of the suspect. These descriptions serve a dual purpose. First they are used to see whether they match with the appearance of the suspect. Second they are used to define the set of people from which foils will be selected.

With respect to the first usage the following is stated in the Devlin Report.

The police usually, but not invariably, obtain and put into writing a description of an unidentified person against whom a complaint is made. It has been suggested to us that such descriptions should be made more fully available than they are at present to the defense before the trial and that they should be admissable in evidence. We recommend that

(1) There should be an administrative rule that the police should, wherever practicable, obtain and put into writing descriptions of an alleged criminal.

(2) The prosecution should be required by statute to supply the defense on request with the name and address of any witness, whether or not he attends a parade, who is known to them as having seen the criminal in the circumstances of the crime, together with a copy of the description, if any, of the criminal given by such a person.

(3) When a witness for the prosecution has identified in court the accused as a person whom he saw in the circumstances of the crime, any written description of that person, signed by that witness and given when first interviewed by a police officer, should by statute be made admissable in evidence to show that the witness's identification is consistent with the description as given. (pp. 151–52).

The last clause is of especial interest because it suggests that a prior description of the criminal which is at odds with the outer appearance of the suspect may exclude the witness who produced the description from further identification tests. This rule does not apply of course when it is easy to account for differences with respect to changeable features, like clothing or hairdo.

RULE 17. **Witnesses should, before participation in an identification test, be requested to provide a verbal description of the criminal, as they remember him. These descriptions should be included in the reports of the subsequent identity test.**

RULE 18. **If a prior description is in conflict with the outer**

appearance of the suspect, and the conflict cannot easily be resolved, then it is preferred that the witness who produced the description is excluded from a subsequent identification test.

This last rule is exemplified by a case from my own experience. A man who robbed a supermarket was described as 20 years old, and blond. A suspect was found who was 32 years old, and with black hair. The subsequent attempt at identification should not have been made [De Fouw v. O.M., 1988). In case of doubt it is the court's prerogative to judge whether the discrepancy is acceptable or not.

The use of prior descriptions for the selection of foils will be discussed in a later section.

INSTRUCTIONS

The purpose of an identification procedure should be carefully explained to witnesses. In the words of the Devlin Report it is:

to test the ability of a witness to pick out from a group the person, if he is present, whom the witness has said that he has seen previously on a specified occasion. (p. 151)

From this definition it is clear that the witnesses should not look for every person who looks familiar, or whom they might have met before, but only for the specific person that they encountered in the circumstances of the crime, and of whom a prior verbal description was given.

RULE 19. **The witness should be instructed to identify only one person, viz the person who fits the specific verbal description which was produced by that same witness prior to the test, if he is present in the lineup.**

In principle the witness should inspect the lineup in search of one specific person. If this is not possible, for instance because a witness described two criminals, whereas only one suspect is apprehended who fits both descriptions, it should be possible to ask the witness whether he can identify one of the criminals, but this aspect of the instruction should be described in the later report. The same holds for other deviations in the instruction.

RULE 20. The instruction given to the witness should be literally reported.

The risk of allowing a witness to inspect the parade in search of more than one person is that the witness will confuse different criminals who were all involved in the crime, but who committed different acts and who might be punishable to different degrees. The Devlin Report discusses this situation within the context of exceptional circumstances in which identification could be misleading.

Another example of an exceptional situation arises when the accused does not deny his presence as one of a group at the scene of the crime, but denies that it was he who performed the criminal act, e.g. struck the blow. In such a case visual identification is mixed up with ordinary observation of action in proportions that will vary according to the circumstances. (p. 88)

It was shown in the previous chapter that the number of false positive responses in target-absent lineups is considerably reduced by the presentation of an explicit instruction telling the witnesses that possibly none of the people in the parade is the wanted person. It is not the witnesses' task to make a best guess, but to see whether they can positively identify the person they described. This view is supported by a recommendation of the Devlin committee:

We have been impressed with evidence from psychologists which suggests that witnesses may tend (though the tendency is not apparently reflected in the statistics) to make an identification on parade because they feel that that is what is expected of them. We have considered various ways of relieving the pressure on witnesses of this type and conclude that the best way is for the officer in charge of the parade to tell the witness expressly that the person he saw may not be on the parade. We recommend that this should be done when the officer addresses the witness just before he inspects the parade. (p. 154)

RULE 21. The instruction to the witnesses should stress

that the wanted person is possibly not in the parade or photospread, and that therefore a positive response should be made only when the witness is certain of recognizing that person.

TRAINING OF INVESTIGATORS

The organization and conduct of an identification test is not a task that can be easily performed without thorough training. This training should be concerned with formal procedures such as are presented in this chapter, but also with the avoidance of unconscious suggestion. The Devlin Report specified that for the showing of mugshots the procedure should be supervised by an officer of no less a rank than sergeant. For a live lineup the parade should always be supervised by an inspector or higher.

I do not think that a sufficient amount of training can be guaranteed by a rank in the police organization. What is really relevant is that the police officers responsible for the organization and conduct of identification tests should have demonstrably received the necessary training. The proof should not only reside in the formal reception of training, but also in the quality of the actual execution of the identification procedure and in the written and oral testimony presented to the court.

RULE 22. **Police officers in charge of identification procedures should have received the appropriate training and should be able to demonstrate their professional qualifications both in written and oral testimony.**

COMPOSITION OF THE PARADE

When witnesses are misinformed about the number of suspects in the parade, they might shift their response criterion in an undesirable manner. Therefore it is necessary to tell witnesses that a parade contains only one suspect, and that they are not allowed to point to more than one person in the parade.

RULE 23. **A parade or photospread should not contain more than one suspect.**

RULE 24. **Witnesses should be instructed that there is only one suspect in the lineup. If they describe more suspects to the police, they should be told which of these suspects they are asked to identify.**

RULE 25. **If there are more suspects who are to be identified by the same witness, it is necessary to organize separate parades for each suspect. Such successive parade should never contain foils that were shown to the witness in a previous parade.**

RULE 26. **Witnesses should be instructed that they are not allowed to point to more than one person in the parade.**

The scientific literature does not provide clear indications about the number of foils that need to be included in a live identity parade. The Devlin Report specifies that there should be at least 12 photos in a mugfile inspection. Israeli law requires 8 photos. But it is not clear whether the same numbers hold for photospreads and for live lineups. Because of the difficulty of finding plausible foils, lineup sizes such as 10 or 12 will be impracticable in some cases. The literature does not discuss in an approving manner lineups with less than 6 people, which could mean that there is a silent agreement about 6 as the minimum accepted lineup size. However, it has been reported that the risk of false positive responses in target-absent lineups is reduced considerably when the lineup size increases to 10 or 12. Therefore, although it is difficult to support this by scientific research, I have a strong preference for the large lineup sizes.

RULE 27. **Identity parades should not contain less than 6 people, and preferably 10 to 12 people.**

The selection of foils should be based on the prior description or descriptions given by witnesses (cf. Rule 17). This leads to the following rule.

RULE 28. **All foils in an identity test should fit the prior descriptions obtained from witnesses.**

Descriptions that do not fit the appearance of the suspect cannot be used for foil selection because it would lead to a systematic difference between the suspect and the foils. For example, when a criminal is described as blond, while the suspect is darkhaired, it would be wrong to select blond foils and to place the darkhaired suspect in a row of blond foils. In such a case it would be wise to discard not only the statement that the criminal was blond, but the whole prior description by that witness. This is expressed in the following rule.

RULE 29. **Prior descriptions of the criminal that do not fit the suspect's appearance cannot be used for selection of foils.**

The effect of rejecting faulty prior descriptions could be that there is no description left on which the selection of foils can be based. In that case, it will be very difficult to conduct a lineup test because, according to Rule 18, there would also be no witness who can be tested. Moreover, one is forced to select foils on the basis of arbitrary criteria not inferred from a prior description.

RULE 30. **An identity test should be interpreted with the requisite prudence when there is not at least one prior description that fits the suspect.**

The Devlin Report specifies that foils should not be selected from an extremely restricted or homogeneous group, such as prisoners, police officers, or the army, because the result might be that the foils share a feature that is not present in the suspect. An example is the case reported in Chapter 2, where the foils were policemen with black service shoes, while the suspect was wearing sneakers.

Rule 31. **Members of a homogeneous group, such as the police, should not normally be used as participants in an identification parade (Devlin Report, p. 153).**

The objective of a proper selection of foils is to compose a lineup or photospread from which only a witness who remembers the individual features of the criminal can pick him out, if he is present at all. For others, it should be impossible to do so; they should either refuse to point at anyone in the parade, or their responses should be distributed evenly over all participants. In order to achieve this objective, it is necessary that foils are selected such that others, for instance mock witnesses, will not find a single cue that helps them to guess who is the suspect.

RULE 32. Foils should be selected such that others, who have not been witnesses to the crime, will find no cues that help them to guess who is the suspect.

The requirement of an even spread of choices of mock witnesses dictates that there should also be no cues suggesting that a foil is *not* the suspect. Examples would be the use of a humpback who otherwise fits the description, or the use of a person well known to the witness. Sometimes it happens that police officers serve as foils, while the witness had opportunity to see these men before in the police station. This aspect of fairness is not easily tested with mock witnesses because the familiarity of a foil could be limited to the real witness.

RULE 33. Foils should be selected such that witnesses will find no cues that help them to guess that a foil is not the suspect.

During the course of litigation it is often necessary to check the fair selection of foils. To that end it is necessary to present photographic recordings of a live identity parade. These recordings should be made available to the defense so that a test of lineup fairness can be conducted, for instance through the use of mock witnesses. I do not think that police investigators should be forced to measure the fairness of their identification tests as a matter of routine, but when fairness is challenged, it should be possible to perform post hoc tests.

RULE 34. The actual material used for photo identification tests should be kept for later inspection and should automatically be given to the defense. The record should reflect the

order in which photos were shown, or the arrangement of the photos as they were shown.

Photographing of live parades was also recommended by the Devlin Committee:

It has been proposed to us that the parade should be photographed so that the jury may have an opportunity of judging for itself whether or not the suspect stands out. Objections of some weight have been made to the taking of a photograph and, accordingly, we recommend that experiments should first be made in a number of representative areas and that, unless they prove unsuccessful, the practice of taking a photograph should be made universal. (p. 154)

This was said in 1976. There is sufficient experience now to conclude that there are no practical objections to the taking of photographs.

RULE 35. **Live identity parades should be recorded on photographs. These recordings should automatically be given to the defense.**

Since photographs of a lineup may fail to reveal some aspects of the actual situation, the request is sometimes made for a repetition of the live parade. Therefore it is necessary to record names and addresses of the foils.

RULE 36. **Names and addresses of participants in the parade should be recorded, but not automatically given to the accused. They may be given to the defense on request (Devlin Report, p. 153).**

Differences between suspect and foils are not only created by their outer appearance, but also by their behavior at the parade: facial expression, pose, and gesture can all betray the identity of suspect or foils. In the case of photo identity parades such hidden cues can be detected at a later stage, but for live lineups this will be impossible unless a video recording of the test is made.

RULE 37. **It is advised that video recordings of live lineup tests should be made whenever it is possible.**

In order to minimize the risk that suspects or foils will transmit information through facial expression, etc., it is necessary to instruct all participants carefully not to do so.

RULE 38. Participants in a lineup should be instructed how to behave.

The literature on live lineups versus the use of photographic stills indicates that the difference with respect to reliability is marginal. The advantage of using stills is that influence of facial expression and gesture can be reduced, while the actual presentation remains open to later inspection. The advantage of a live identity parade is that witnesses could be allowed to see some participants walk, or even to hear their voices. The Devlin Report provides some guidelines for such practices, but I feel that they should in principle be avoided. When witnesses do not recognize the suspect at first sight, they should not be allowed to base an uncertain judgment on unreliable cues such as gait or voice. Therefore it could be argued that the best method is to arrange a live lineup, to photograph it, and to present only the photograph to witnesses. I will not formulate this preference in a rule, since the use of live identity parades is certainly not rejected.

A substantial obstacle to identification is the transformation of the criminal that may take place between the crime and the test. It is sometimes possible to restore such transformations. In my own experience, I have dealt with a case in which a bank robber was wearing a wig with long curls. It was decided to give similar wigs to all participants in the lineup to minimize transformation. The same could be done with headgear, masks, clothing, sunglasses, etc. A difference of age can create a problem, especially in cases like those of De Rijke and Demjanjuk, where more than 30 years have gone by. In such cases it would be reasonable to reduce transformation through the use of photographs taken in the period of the crime. The reduction of transformation effects would certainly outweigh the marginal disadvantages of photographic stills.

RULE 39. Transformations occurring in the period between

the crime and the identification test should be counteracted as much as possible.

UNCONSCIOUS SUGGESTION

It is difficult to prevent unconscious suggestion if the investigator knows which person in the lineup is the suspect. A nod, a slight holding of one's breath, might be sufficient to give away essential information. The Supreme Court of the United States gave as its opinion that

the influence of improper suggestion upon identifying witnesses probably accounts for more miscarriages of justice than any other single factor – perhaps it is responsible for more such errors than all other factors combined (cf. Malpass and Devine, 1984).

A reasonable way to prevent such effects is to have the identification test administered by an investigator who is unaware of who the suspect is. The Devlin Report says about this issue:

While it is desirable that a suspect should always have a solicitor representing him at the parade, this is not an indispensable requirement. If, however, the accused's solicitor is not present the officer investigating the case should be excluded from the parade. (p. 153)

The actual administration of the test can be conducted in most cases by a police officer who does not know who the suspect is. The exception would be a case in which there are many witnesses. After consistent identifications by a number of witnesses the police officer would have formed his own opinion, right or wrong, that could exert an influence on the remaining witnesses. But in practice this problem might not occur because there is no point in the subsequent testing of a large number of witnesses (see Rule 13).

RULE 40. **Whenever it is possible, identification tests should be administered by police officers who do not know which person in the lineup is the suspect.**

Another preventive measure is the strict timing of the

procedure. The showing of photographs or the presentation of a live parade should be limited to a number of minutes, not more. An immediate recognition does not require longer than that; a longer inspection time would only invite guessing. A variation of inspection time, left to the discretion of the investigator, would introduce an extra opportunity for unconscious suggestion.

RULE 41. **The presentation of photographs or live parades should be strictly limited to a preset time period, and the witnesses should be informed about this.**

A further check on unconscious suggestion is the exact recording of what happened. The best way of doing this is by means of a video recording, such as suggested in Rule 37, or tape recording. Next best is the production of a stenographic transcript, supplemented with a time log. The worst is a statement drafted after the identification test is completed. Almost without exception police investigators around the world resort to the last solution. The Devlin Report does not say much about this issue. The only recommendation is: 'Any observation volunteered by the witness should be recorded' (p. 153). A post hoc statement would not guarantee that even this minimal requirement is fulfilled. But I feel that a much stricter regime is called for since it is essential that a court ascertains that the identifications were not influenced by unconscious suggestions of the investigators.

RULE 42. **All relevant details of the preparation and conduct of identification tests should be recorded.**

One way that suggestions can be transmitted to the witness is by giving them feedback on whether they selected the suspect or a foil. In the first case they might tend to strengthen their statement by further additions like 'I am 100 percent certain, I will never forget this face, I am sure because I remember those ears'. Such statements could reflect a degree of certainty that did not exist before but that was elicited by positive feedback. When witnesses are told that they identified a foil, they might weaken their statement by saying 'Well, I wasn't sure anyway', which reduces the information contained in a false positive. At worst they could be allowed to retract their identification and make a second guess. This would, of course, be in conflict with Rule 26, which states that witnesses may pick out one participant only. Another disadvantage of feedback is that witnesses might tell other witnesses about their success, and even who the suspect is.

RULE 43. **Witnesses should not be given feedback with respect to whether they identified the suspect or a foil.**

Finally it would be possible to check the use of unconscious suggestion through the presence of a defense counsel. This issue will be discussed in the next section.

PRESENCE OF DEFENSE COUNSEL

The presence of defense counsel was already mentioned in the context of Rule 11. There the issue was the failure to report unsuccessful identifications. But there is more at stake than selective reporting or unconscious suggestion. The real issue is that an identification parade is not only an important element of evidence against a suspect, but also an important means of vindicating the defendant. The Devlin Report mentions that in about 50 percent of the recorded cases witnesses do not identify the suspect. In reality this proportion will be even larger because there will be an excess of failed identifications in the unreported cases. Identification tests cannot be repeated once they have taken place (see Rule 7). Violations of rules will promote the incrimination of the accused, rather than increasing the demonstrability of innocence. Even if an improperly conducted test is later rejected by the court, it could be that a valuable opportunity of vindicating the accused was lost. When there is a scarcity of witnesses, it is therefore in the interest of the defendant that the identification tests are performed according to the rules. The presence of defense counsel is one way to ensure this.

The Devlin Report states only that it is 'desirable that a suspect should always have a solicitor representing him at a parade.' In the State of Israel it is required by statute. In the light of the foregoing I think that it is eminently important that the accused is allowed the assistance of defense counsel at parades, and that a refusal of this elementary right should be justified by the investigators in the written report.

RULE 44. Defense counsel should be given the right to attend identification tests.

RESEMBLANCE OR IDENTITY?

An identification test is in principle conducted in order to prove the identity between the suspect and the wanted criminal. Therefore witnesses should be asked to pronounce a judgment about identity, not about resemblance. The question is 'Which of these people *is* the criminal you saw', not 'Which of these people *resembles* the criminal'. Responses phrased as 'This man resembles. . . This man reminds me. . . This man has the posture of. . .' should not be accepted as positive identifications. Or, in the words of the Devlin Report:

The device of the parade eliminates the uncertain witnesses. It does no more than that. . . (p. 152)

However, the literature presented in Chapter 2 has clearly indicated that uncertain witnesses are hardly less likely to be correct. Uncertainty in itself is not a predictor of low accuracy. The real issue is whether the process of identification was immediate and direct, as in the case of recognizing one's neighbor, or more like a delayed and indirect reconstruction on the basis of a perceived resemblance. We have seen that such reconstructions may result in high levels of confidence, even when they are incorrect. The objective of identification tests should be to keep the direct recognitions and to eliminate the reconstructions. Indicators of reconstruction processes are such explicit statements of uncertainty as mentioned above and extremely long inspection times.

In some cases a statement of resemblance could have some probative value. The Devlin Report cites a case which depended mainly on circumstantial evidence and in which witnesses could only confirm that the suspect resembled the criminal because they did not have a clear view of the criminal during the crime. Relying on other evidence mainly, the court might want to be told whether or not the suspect resembles the criminal. But in general uncertain identifications should be classified as failures.

Identifications that take an extremely long time are already excluded when the timing of the procedure is strict, such as suggested in Rule 41. This will also help to eliminate uncertain responses. When Rule 41 is not followed, it will be wise to reject identifications that were given after a very long inspection period. Recognition is usually something that 'jumps into the eye'. Inspection times beyond several minutes reflect uncertainty, and uncertain testimony should not be accepted. Other indications of uncertainty, e.g. remarks like 'It has been a long time', or 'It all looks different now', can in principle lead to a rejection of the identification. These considerations lead to the following rules.

RULE 45. **Identifications should not be accepted as evidence when witnesses declare to see only a resemblance.**

RULE 46. **Full recognitions pronounced only after a considerable time should not be accepted as positive identifications.**

Rule 47. **Other expressions of uncertainty on the part of the witness should be recorded, and may lead to a rejection of the identification.**

DOCK IDENTIFICATIONS

The identification of a suspect while sitting in the dock should be avoided because this procedure violates most of the rules presented above. Dock identification is usually a showup, not a lineup. It is possible to place the accused among the jury or the general public, but even that would not conform to the requirements of a well-controlled identification test. In many cases dock identifications are repetitions of proper identification tests conducted by the investigators. The Devlin Report concluded about this:

> It is generally agreed that dock identification is undesirable and unsatisfactory. . . Identification on parade or in some other similar way in which the witness takes the initiative in picking out the accused should be made a condition to be dispensed with only when the holding of a parade would have been impracticable or unnecessary. An example of its being impracticable is when the accused refuses to attend. An example of its being unnecessary is when the accused is already well known to the witness. (p. 150)

The two examples stated by the Report are unconvincing. A refusal to attend a live lineup does not preclude the use of photographic stills. We have seen before that the results of photographic lineups are only marginally less reliable than those of live lineups. There is definitely no reason to prefer dock identifications, which are notoriously unreliable, to photographic identification tests. The other example, the suspect that is well-known to the witness, is even more questionable. When the witness knows the accused well, the question is not whether the witness can recognize him, but only whether the witness was correct when he reported the involvement of the accused. This cannot be established by means of a lineup or a dock identification. The Devlin Committee proposed that dock identification should be permitted in a limited number of circumstances, and this introduced a rather complicated statutory provision. I feel that there are good grounds to dismiss dock identification entirely. Dock identifications, as a matter of course, exist as a necessary step in the judicial procedure. But then it is purely formal, and no one objects to it as a matter of form. But a court or jury should not confuse this formality with a proper identification test.

RULE 48. **Dock identifications can never be accepted as proof of identity.**

BREACH OF RULES

The rules presented above have the intention of reducing the risks involved in the identification of people by eyewitnesses. There is no doubt that mistaken identification is a major source of wrong convictions. The Devlin Report presented the following opinions, and these have been augmented by many other authoritative bodies.

The CLRC [Criminal Law Review Committee] in its Eleventh Report, paragraph 196 said: 'We regard mistaken identification as by far the greatest cause of actual or possible wrong convictions.' There has been a number of judicial dicta to the like effect. Many English judges, although they have not gone so far as the Supreme Court of the Republic of Ireland, which has laid it down that in all cases where the verdict depends substantially on the correctness of an identification the jury must be specially warned, have noted that identification cases are always difficult and a cause for anxiety. In October 1974 Lord Justice Scarman in the Court of Appeal spoke of 'the vexed question of how the court should deal with identification evidence', and later: 'We all know there is no branch of human perception more fallible than identifying a person.' The Lord Chief Justice in an address to the Magistrates' Association in October 1974 referred to it as 'perhaps the most serious chink in our armour'. Sir Norman Shelton, the Director of Public Prosecutions in his evidence to us called it 'the Achilles heel of British justice'. (p. 75)

In view of the size of our problem it is obvious that rules for the conduct and interpretation of identification tests are needed, and that a breach of rules should in principle lead to the rejection of the evidence. The Devlin Report says about parade rules:

If the trial judge considers that a breach of the rules (or any other piece of misconduct or misfortune) has made the test unsatisfactory the parade or the part of it affected should by statute be treated as a nullity and any evidence that emerges out of it should be excluded. (p. 151)

In case of a dispute about the rules, for instance because the rules cannot be easily implemented in a specific case, there should at least be a justification for violation of the rules in the written report so that the court or the jury can decide whether the result of the identification test is still acceptable as legal evidence. The Devlin Report says:

There may, however, be cases (we have come across only a few) in which there is a genuine dispute between the police and the defense about the conditions under which the parade should be held. . . If deadlock is reached, the defense should submit under protest and take their objection at the trial. The result would be that if the conditions were such as to defeat the object of the parade, it would be treated as a nullity. (p. 154)

These considerations lead to the following rule.

RULE 49. **A breach of rules, when not justified in the written report, should lead to a rejection of an identification test.**

Violation of rules is not equally fatal for all rules. But there is a limited set of rules that should not be violated under any circumstance because they are at the heart of the logic underlying identification tests, and because the violations cannot be repaired once they have occurred. Such violations should automatically lead to a rejection of the identification test, irrespective of whether a justification is provided. In my opinion there are 23 of these rules: the numbers 1, 3, 4, 7, 14, 17, 18, 19, 21, 23–33, 38, 41, and 42. Violations of the other rules can sometimes be accepted on the basis of specific aspects of a case, or be repaired afterwards. But, since identification tests cannot be repeated, violation of rules should lead to a rejection of the test when the essence of the test is affected. This consideration leads to the last rule in this chapter.

RULE 50. **When it is shown that violation of a rule has reduced the validity of a test by a substantial degree, it should be decided to reject the test, even when the violation is justified in the written report.**

A number of these rules are meant to assist the court or the jury, not the investigators. Examples are Rules 8 and 9, which both relate to the corroboration needed for acceptance of eyewitness identification as proof, and Rules 49 and 50, about violations of the rules. It would not be proper to present such rules as prescriptive for a court or jury because decisions about the acceptance of identifications have to be made separately for each case. But all advice to courts and juries can be based on the observation of the Devlin Report that eyewitness identification is inherently unreliable, and that the most effective protection against mistakes is by increasing the burden of proof (pp. 149–50). Thus a large share in the responsibility is taken from the investigators and put in the hands of the court or the jury. This responsibility can be realized by considering some of the rules presented in this chapter.

CONCLUSION

The rules presented in this chapter are not cast in the form of statutory law. Legal experts might find much wrong in the formulations. But taken together with the supporting literature, it is obvious what the objectives of these rules are. Whether the objectives are achieved through exactly these rules or others is immaterial. What counts is that identification tests need to conform to a number of procedural restrictions if their results are to be accepted as legal evidence. The next two chapters, in which the case of John Demjanjuk is described, will demonstrate how identification tests are administered in practice when the investigators are not aware of all rules.

4 The Identification of John Demjanjuk

PREPARATION OF THE INVESTIGATIONS

Early in 1976, the Israeli police, Nazi Crime Investigation Division, received a collection of 17 photographs from the United States Immigration and Naturalization Service known as INS. The 17 photographs were of Ukrainians living in the United States who were suspected of Nazi crimes. The Israelis were asked to find witnesses in Israel who were able to tell more about these Ukranians and who could possibly identify them in the photospread.

The pictures were pasted on three cardboard pages by the Israeli police. I will refer to this collection as 'the album'. The album pictures could only be shown page by page as it was impossible to make any special selection or to rearrange the pictures. In the second half of May 1976 three more pages were added to the album, but they were, as far as we know, not used in the investigation. With the pictures came a list of names and a short description of the accusation. The investigation was placed in the hands of Mrs. Radiwker, of the Israeli police. She decided to start with the suspects Fedorenko and Demjanjuk because they had allegedly been guards in, respectively, Treblinka and Sobibor. She expected that it would be extremely difficult to find people to bear witness against the other suspects. Page three of the album is reproduced in this book. It shows the pictures with numbers 10–17. No. 16 is the immigration picture of John Demjanjuk, taken in 1951; No. 17 is a picture of Fedorenko.

Mrs. Radiwker started by publishing an advertisement,

inviting survivors of Sobibor and Treblinka to contact her. The Sobibor survivors would be questioned about Demjanjuk, the Treblinka survivors about Fedorenko. But, since the two pictures were pasted on the same page of the album, both groups were to be confronted with the same pictures.

The advertisement was very explicit about Mrs. Radiwker's intentions. It said that:

The Nazi Crime Investigation Division is conducting an investigation against the Ukrainians Ivan Demjanjuk and Fedor Fedorenko. Survivors of the Death Camps at Sobibor and Treblinka are requested to report to the Israel Police Headquarters.

Hence the names of the people to be identified were already known to the witnesses even before the hearings had started.

All album pictures represented Ukrainians suspected of Nazi crimes. No attempts were made to obtain pictures of innocent foils, nor to standardize the available pictures with respect to size, part of the body shown, or sharpness. As a consequence there was a great variety. The two pictures of Demjanjuk and Fedorenko were the largest on their page, and the face of Demjanjuk was even larger than Fedorenko's.

The procedure adopted by Mrs. Radiwker was to interview the witnesses before showing the photospread. The witnesses testified in Hebrew. Mrs. Radiwker wrote a statement of their testimony only at the end of the hearing, from her memory. The statement was written in the German language, and then read to the witnesses in Hebrew, after which the witnesses signed every page. This procedure does, of course, not guarantee a maximum of accuracy, and disputes about what was really said frequently arose in court. A general overview of the identification tests, which were administered between May 1976 and February 1981, is presented in Table 4.1.

Figure 4.1: Page 3 of the album. No. 16 is Demjanjuk, No. 17 is Fedorenko.

Table 4.1: A general overview of the identification tests in the Demjanjuk case

Date	Names	Cases	Spread
May 1976	Turowski Goldfarb	Both questioned about Fedorenko and Demjanjuk	Album
May 1976	Rosenberg	Demjanjuk	Album
June 1976	Teigman, Kudlik	Both questioned about Fedorenko and Demjanjuk	Album
July/ August 1976	Greenspan, Freiberg Cohen Engleman Seiss	All questioned about Fedorenko and Demjanjuk	Album
September/ October 1976	Czarny Helman Boraks Lindwasser	All questioned about Fedorenko and Demjanjuk	Album
March 1978	Epstein	Questioned about Fedorenko and Demjanjuk	Album
April 1978	Rosenberg	Fedorenko	Album
December 1979	Epstein	Demjanjuk	Trawniki
December 1979	Rosenberg	Demjanjuk	Trawniki
March 1980	Rajchman	Demjanjuk	OSI
March 1980	Rajchman	Demjanjuk	Trawniki
February 1981	Boraks	Demjanjuk	Trawniki
February 1981	Boraks	Demjanjuk	Album

THE TESTIMONIES OF TUROWSKI AND GOLDFARB

The first two witnesses in the case of John Demjanjuk, Eugen Turowski and Abraham Goldfarb, were questioned by Mrs. Radiwker on May 9 and 10, 1976. A summary of the proceedings is presented in Table 4.2.

Table 4.2: The identifications by Turowski and Goldfarb in May 1976

Date	Time	Name	Case	Result
May 9, 1976	10 am	Eugen Turowski	Fedorenko	Identified Fedorenko. No mention of Ivan.
May 9, 1976	1 pm	Abraham Goldfarb	Fedorenko	No recognition of Fedorenko. Picture No. 16 'seems familiar'. No mention of Ivan.
May 9, 1976	2.30 pm	Abraham Goldfarb	Demjanjuk	'I believe I recognize Ivan'.
May 10, 1976	12 am	Eugen Turowski	Demjanjuk	'I know the name Demjanjuk'. 'Him I recognize immediately'.

The events of May 9 are especially relevant for a correct understanding of what happened. At 10 o'clock in the morning Turowski was interviewed in the case against Fedorenko. Since he was a Treblinka survivor, there was no reason to ask him about Demjanjuk. The written statement says:

According to my memory in Treblinka were about 80 Ukrainians as personnel. If asked about the names of the Ukrainians, so I can in reality mention the name of only one Ukrainian, who had a ring, whom I knew. The simple guards did not come to the workshops, and I had nothing to do with them. The Ukrainian called Fedorenko I knew personally. He was an underofficer, and I saw him almost daily. I knew him by his name, and as I said, also personally.

Further on it says:

The witness was shown 17 photos of Ukrainian nazi criminals, glued on three brown carton pages. The witness declares: The man on photo No. 17 (photo of Fedorenko) is known to me. The witness looks in more detail on the photo and declares: This could be Fedorenko, I am almost certain, but I must point out only that I have always seen him in uniform and here he is in civilian clothing. Most of the time on Sundays and holidays he had a black uniform, and every other day a khaki uniform always with a sailor cap. As said, he was an underofficer. If now I look for more time on the photo I can say: this is Fedorenko, I am certain of it.

It should be realized that, while Turowski was inspecting picture 17, Demjanjuk's picture was adjacent to it all the time. Turowski did not refer to it with one word on May 9. Or rather the written statement does not mention such a reference. At 1.00 p.m. Goldfarb was questioned by Mrs. Radiwker, also on Fedorenko. He declared:

I do not remember an Ukrainian by the name of Fedorenko, that is, I do not remember the name Fedorenko. I was shown 17 photos of Ukrainians pasted on three brown cardboard pages. The man on picture No. 16 seems familiar to me. When asked about it: I cannot identify the man on picture No. 17, which should be a representation of Fedorenko.

Thus, at one o'clock in the afternoon Goldfarb seemed to recognize Demjanjuk. This was the first time a relation between Demjanjuk and Treblinka was suggested, although Goldfarb did not mention the name Ivan. Goldfarb was heard again on the same day, at 2.30 p.m. His second statement starts with:

To the subject of investigations against the Ukrainian Nazi criminal Demjanjuk, Ivan, Mr. Abraham Goldfarb was given a hearing today.

Apart from the fact that Mrs. Radiwker appears to assume already that Demjanjuk is a criminal, instead of a suspect, the statement suggests that the name Ivan was mentioned before the testimony started. We do not know this for sure because the written statement is not a literal transcript of what was said. But since Mrs. Radiwker saw no harm in reporting it this way, we may infer that she would have seen no harm in such a procedure. Before the identification Goldfarb declared:

To the question: I don't remember the names of the Ukrainians—the name of Demjanjuk I don't recall. I do remember a Ukrainian whose first name was Ivan. He may have been 23–24 years old, was rather tall, had a full, round face. He wore a black uniform, a seaman's cap, he had no rank, I didn't see a rank insignia on him.

This statement can only mean that Mrs. Radiwker asked Goldfarb something like: 'Do you recognize the name Ivan Demjanjuk?', although the written statement does not mention this question. Therefore we cannot distinguish between the spontaneous and prompted mentioning of names in Mrs. Radiwker's reports. The description of Ivan's face could have been taken from memory, but it is equally possible that Goldfarb is simply describing the picture he saw an hour before. The identification runs as follows:

On the 17 photos shown to me, I believe I recognize this Ivan on picture No. 16. When you tell me that this Ukrainian was allegedly in Trawniki and Sobibor, I can say that during 1942/1943 he had to be in Treblinka, but before the uprising in the summer of 1943, he was no longer, I believe, in Treblinka. The man depicted on picture 16, I remember from the gas chambers. His function at the gas chambers was, together with a German SS-man, the 'machinist' of the gas chamber whose name I have forgotten, to release the gas from the Diesel motor into the gas chambers.

The reference to Sobibor is revealing. Again the statement does not contain Mrs. Radiwker's question, but apparently she told Goldfarb that he made a mistake, because her files related Demjanjuk to Sobibor, not to Treblinka. But now Goldfarb is certain that No. 16 depicts Ivan; much more certain than he was at 1.00 p.m., when he said: 'Seems familiar to me'. Why was he so certain now? Had he forgotten the name of Ivan, and did the prompting by Mrs. Radiwker cue him into memories that were not released before by looking at Demjanjuk's picture? Or did he recognize the picture because he had looked at it an hour ago? We will never know exactly what happened, because Goldfarb died in 1984, while Mrs. Radiwker remained very vague in her later explanations.

Turowski was asked to appear again on the next day, May 10, 1976. Now he was questioned about Ivan, apparently in order to verify the unexpected statement of Goldfarb, which seemed to contradict the information provided by INS. The statement says:

When asked if I knew an Ukrainian by the name of Demjanjuk, Ivan, I declare as follows: I know the name Demjanjuk and even better, the first name of Ivan. To me, he was Ivan. This Ukrainian I can well remember, I knew him personally, because at times he came to the shop to have things repaired. The witness is shown 17 photographs, all pasted on three brown cardboards. Immediately the witness points at photo No. 16 (photo of Demjanjuk) and declares: This is Ivan. Him I recognize immediately and with full assurance. He was of medium build, stockily built and had a round, full face. He had a short, wide neck and even then his hair looked like here on this photograph, a high forehead with a bald pate starting. He was still a very young man, could have been 23-24 at the most.

This statement obviously creates a puzzle. The previous day Turowski saw the album page with photos No. 16 and 17 next to each other. He recognized No. 17, but failed to mention Ivan on No. 16. The following day, after Mrs. Radiwker mentioned the name Ivan, he recognized Ivan immediately and with full assurance. Of course Mrs. Radiwker was confronted with this paradoxical situation in court. She stated that the immediate and certain recognition by Turowski had in fact occurred already on May 9. He had been very excited and had cried: 'This is Ivan, this is Ivan'. Mrs. Radiwker had been so shocked by the idea that the American information could be wrong, that she did not want to pursue this line, and she sent Turowski home after taking the statement about Demjanjuk. When Goldfarb also happened to recognize Ivan, she had decided to open up another line of investigation and to summon Turowski again. The following discussion between the defense counsel cross examining Mrs. Radiwker in the Jerusalem court illustrates how unsatisfactory this explanation is.

Q. Now you told us later on in your testimony that everything that happened with Mr. Turowski you wrote down in great detail?
A. Yes.
Q. Then could you please explain to me how it is that in none of Turowski's depositions, either on the 9th of May or on the 10th of May—is there any mention of everything you have told us concerning the fact that as soon as you showed him picture No. 16, even though he had been summoned for the Fedorenko case, he was excited, as you say he was. It isn't mentioned on the 9th or on the 10th?
A. On the 9th of May I took from him testimony concerning Fedorenko. On the 10th of May I took testimony concerning Demjanjuk and I reconstructed what had happened on the previous day. (JET, 2828)

This explanation seems at first glance somewhat implausible, as Turowski stated on May 9: 'I can in reality mention the name of only one Ukrainian . . . the Ukrainian Fedorenko'. Not only that the mentioning of Ivan was omitted by Mrs. Radiwker, apparently also an incorrect statement was entered, because, as she claimed afterwards, Turowski knew the name of Ivan as well. The only plausible explanation of this is that Turowski recognized Ivan on May 10 for the first time, and that he failed the day before. The reason why this time order is so important is that the cueing by Mrs. Radiwker played totally different roles on the two different days. On May 9 Mrs. Radiwker did not present any cue related to Ivan, simply because she was investigating Fedorenko, not Demjanjuk. Demjanjuk's picture was a foil, suspected of activities in Sobibor, of which Turowski had no direct knowledge. On the second day the situation was entirely different. Now Mrs. Radiwker was investigating Demjanjuk. She mentioned the name Ivan before the actual identification procedure, she could have given unconscious signals about the target picture, she might even have pointed to picture No. 16 while asking: 'Do you recognize this person?' We know that she asked such questions from Goldfarb's statement about Fedorenko: 'When asked about it, I cannot identify the man on picture No. 17, which should be a representation of Fedorenko.'

The time order is also important if we want to establish the number of independent witnesses. When Turowski and Goldfarb identified Ivan on the same day, it is possible that they did this without having any exchange of information. When Turowski recognized him on the next day, as the official documents say, it cannot be discounted that Goldfarb told him about it. The two witnesses knew each other, and Goldfarb had much more reason than Mrs. Radiwker to be shocked by his discovery, especially because Goldfarb was one of those who claimed that Ivan was killed in the uprising.

Another riddle in Turowski's second statement is that he claimed to know the name Demjanjuk. None of the other witnesses knew Ivan's last name. The connection between

John Demjanjuk and Ivan the Terrible is through the recognition by eyewitnesses, not through the correspondence of last names. The statement is even more surprising in view of the fact that Turowski had already said that he remembered no other name than Fedorenko. Mrs. Radiwker had clearly mentioned the name Demjanjuk before Turowski claimed to recognize it, hence the recall was not at all spontaneous. Still it would be essential to the case for one witness to testify that Ivan's last name was really Demjanjuk. But how could Turowski have known this name? Mrs. Radiwker was asked about this. She answered: 'It did not interest me.' Obviously she missed the vital point: that Turowski's ready agreement that he knew the name mentioned to him, although in fact he probably did not know it, might signify that he was sensitive to suggestions made by the investigator.

The least that is clear from the riddles in these first testimonies is that Mrs. Radiwker's reports are highly inaccurate. It is likely that Goldfarb identified Ivan spontaneously, but with respect to Turowski there must be doubts.

ROSENBERG'S TESTIMONIES

One day later, on May 11, the third witness, Elijahu Rosenberg, was questioned about Demjanjuk. He had not testified on Fedorenko before, and had therefore not seen the album pictures. He pointed at picture No. 16 and declared:

I see a great resemblance to the Ukrainian Ivan, who was active in camp 2, and who was called 'Ivan Grozny' (Ivan the Terrible). It is the same face construction, he had a round full face, around the eyes and forehead. He had a high forehead with the beginning of baldness, at any rate, a very high forehead and very short hair. He had a short, thick neck, stocky build and swarthy skin. I remember that his ears were standing away from his face. I decline, however, to identify him with absolute certainty. He was very young, maybe 22–23 years old.

The identification by Rosenberg was a surprise because in several official documents he had testified that Ivan had been killed during the uprising. In 1947 he declared in Vienna, on his way to Israel:

After this, some of the people ran into the barracks where Ukrainian guards were sleeping, among them was Ivan, and killed them with shovels. These men had the night shift and were very tired, so that they did not wake up quickly enough.

Of course Rosenberg was, when he testified in court, questioned about this statement. He explained that Friedman, the interrogator in the small Vienna Documentation Center, had misrepresented his words. He had actually said that, after his escape from Treblinka, some others had *told* him that Ivan was killed. He had not himself seen it happening. However, in January 1988 a handwritten statement by Rosenberg dated 1945 was discovered in a Warsaw archive. This statement referred to the death of Ivan as something witnessed by Rosenberg himself. Confronted with this statement Rosenberg declared: 'It was a dream, a strong desire, I wanted it to be true. Now I know that Ivan is still alive.'

Another problem with Rosenberg's identification stems from a later statement, made in 1978. On April 13, 1978 Rosenberg was interviewed by Mrs. Radiwker's successor, Mr. Kolar, in the case against Fedorenko. He was shown the one album page with the pictures of Fedorenko and Demjanjuk. The question was: 'Do you recognize any of these people?' Rosenberg pointed at Fedorenko and said: 'This picture reminds me of some of the guards in the Ukrainian staff at the Treblinka camp.' There is no reference to a recognition of Demjanjuk, and there was no reference to Fedorenko in the 1976 testimony that involved the same pictures. In the cross examination Rosenberg declared:

I was summoned to Mr. Kolar, to identify pictures in an album, a certain album, after he asked me where I had been. He showed me this album. When I opened the album my first word was: 'Sir, you brought me here again? I've pointed to Ivan already.' And he said, 'No, we're not talking about Ivan. Look well. Look carefully, and tell me who you see here, who else you see.' I looked, I looked for a long time and I pointed to a certain picture if it was 17 or 22, but I pointed to a certain picture and I said, 'This man, this man,' your honor, I pointed and I said 'This man' after I had said Ivan is here I said 'This man I know from Treblinka and I know him from elsewhere too.' (United States v. Fedorenko, 1978)

This statement illustrates quite clearly the sort of problem created by the procedures used by the Israeli investigators. The habit of phrasing a statement after the event creates an opportunity to leave out facts that in a later stage appear to be crucial. Rosenberg claims that his identification of Ivan in 1978 was completely omitted. The statement, if true, may also reveal a certain degree of coaching or guiding on the part of the interrogator. Rosenberg identifies Ivan, and Kolar says: 'No, . . . who else?' How many other identifications were rejected before Rosenberg hit on Fedorenko? And how many identifications were made before he hit on Ivan? This sort of guidance is, of course, wholly illegitimate and does not appear at all in the official documents.

In 1981, during the trial conducted in Cleveland, which removed Demjanjuk's citizenship, and which resulted in his extradition to Israel, Rosenberg gave a completely different account of the event.

Q. Mr. Rosenberg, do you remember when you were first interviewed in Israel in connection with this case?
A. Yes.
Q. Do you remember approximately when this was?
A. It would be about four years ago, I think.
Q. And with whom did you speak?
A. A woman in the police station.
Q. At that time were you shown any photographs?
A. No.
Q. Did there come a time, do you recall, being shown photographs?
A. Yes. She had got in touch with me on the telephone. I told her that I'm prepared to look at them, but she would have to come to me in my office where I work. One day I made an appointment with her, and she came.
Q. Did she show you photographs?
A. First she asked me all kinds of questions.
—————
Q. Did you recognize any of the photographs?
A. Yes. At that time I identified two pictures.
Q. And who were these two pictures – who was in these two pictures that you identified?
A. One picture, I said 'This man, I don't remember his name.' The other picture I recalled, and I said 'This man is very, very close in appear-

ance to a Ukrainian whose name is Ivan, and he was in Treblinka.'
(United States of America v. Demjanjuk, Cleveland, 1981)

Now it appears that Rosenberg saw Mrs. Radiwker before the session on May 11, but there is no reference to this meeting in any official document. What happened then? What did Mrs. Radiwker tell Rosenberg about the case? The other surprising fact is that Rosenberg declares, under oath, that he identified two people right from the beginning. Since this testimony was made in 1981, an explanation of the discrepancy could be that, after five years, he simply confused the 1976 and 1978 interviews. But in 1987, in the Jerusalem trial, he remembered clearly:

When I saw the picture which reminded me of Ivan, I didn't see anything else, I didn't refer to anything else, just about that. That's the only thing that I concentrated on during the few hours that we spent in my office. . . In '76 when I found out he was alive, I was in shock I was in absolute shock. I knew he was alive then, it is him, that he's alive. (JET, 1476)

The story about the shock is not compatible with his 1981 testimony, and not with the phrasing used by Mrs. Radiwker in 1976: 'I see a great resemblance; I decline to identify with full certainty.' It is at least problematic that in 1981 Rosenberg should confuse the two identification hearings, while in 1987 his memory returned with so much vividness. It is even worse that Rosenberg's statements, made in the Jerusalem court, do not square at all with the official account defended by Mrs. Radiwker in the same court.

Kolar, the investigator at the 1978 session, was also asked about the event. He declared that Rosenberg certainly had not at first made such an explicit reference to Ivan and his previous testimony. Even more to the point, in the trial against Fedorenko, also in 1978, Kolar was asked whether Rosenberg also pointed to other photographs. At that time Kolar replied:

Mr. Rosenberg is a careful and prudent and judicious person, he only answers questions to him and he did not point to any other person and did not mention anyone else. (JET, 3236)

After a careful inspection of Rosenberg's 1987 testimony Kolar stated:

> This tone, this wording is just not true. Mr. Rosenberg never used this sort of tone in addressing me. (JET, 3240)

Rosenberg's entire testimony is thrown into question. The problem with it has less to do with Rosenberg's memory and more with the inconsistencies in the written testimonies. The attempt to reconcile the contradiction through oral testimony about what really happened during the identification had failed dismally. The additional statements by Rosenberg, Kolar, and Mrs. Radiwker only added contradictions, suggesting that the witnesses might have been subtly coached in an unacceptable manner.

WITNESSES INTERVIEWED IN THE SUMMER AND FALL OF 1976

The questioning of witnesses went on during the summer of 1976, but initially the investigators were not successful. Two witnesses, Teigman and Kudlik, could not identify Demjanjuk nor Fedorenko. Kudlik's interview produced another instance of leading the witness. Counsel for the defense asked Mrs. Radiwker during the cross-examination in Jerusalem:

> Q. Is it true that after these pictures were shown in connection with Fedorenko, and after he did not identify them, you specifically asked him about, or you drew his attention to, picture No. 17, and asked him about No. 17 whether he identifies it or not specifically. And he said that it had been many years and he could not identify?
> A. That's not true.
> Q. That's not true?
> A. I didn't say specifically, look at Fedorenko, or anything like that. I showed pictures the way I always did, just the way I always did. (JET, 2914)

But counsel was reading from the statement written by Mrs. Radiwker herself:

Q. Even when shown the picture of Fedorenko, number 17, the witness
declared: 'It's been a great many years, I always saw the Ukrainian
guards in uniform and hats. They were younger then. I cannot identify
the man in picture No. 17.' Now would you agree with first of all
that, on the basis of what it says here, it emerges that you specifically
pointed to picture No. 17 after in general he did not identify any of
the eight pictures. Is that true?

A. I must have told him, look carefully at picture No. 17. If that is what
it says, that must have been what I did. (JET, 2916)

Again the question emerges, how many of the other
witnesses were coached in the same way?

Simon Greenspan identified Fedorenko on July 4, 1976,
but failed to identify Demjanjuk. This is not unimportant,
because the identification of Fedorenko proves that Greenspan was there, and was able to remember faces. Ivan made
himself much more conspicuous than Fedorenko; how could
Greenspan recognize one but not the other? When asked
about this Mrs. Radiwker said: 'I did not ask him about
Ivan.' But this is no explanation. She testified several times
that she asked all witnesses the same question: 'Do you
recognize any of these people?' No specific name was ever
mentioned, according to her testimony. Greenspan indicated that, although he did not identify Demjanjuk, that he
recognized other guards. Mrs. Radiwker never asked who
these other guards were, because, in her words, 'I questioned him about Fedorenko. He gave me a clear statement
on that. And that was enough.' Apparently she did not feel
that the non-identification of Demjanjuk would be more
significant had Greenspan successfully identified a number
of other guards.

Other unsuccessful witnesses were Dov Freiberg, Shalom
Cohen, Sophia Engleman, and Meir Seiss, but some of them
had not actually been close to Ivan in Treblinka.

The first additional successful identifications were
obtained from September 1976 onwards. This date causes
an obvious problem, as by now the further witnesses could
have talked to Turowski, Goldfarb, or Rosenberg. This is
not at all theoretical, since every year on August 2, the day
of the uprising in Treblinka, some of the survivors used to
meet in Tel Aviv. Turowski, Goldfarb, and Rosenberg all

lived in Israel, as did the witnesses who identified Demjanjuk in September and October: Czarny, Boraks, and Lindwasser. Their testimony can be accepted only after it is established that they did not meet with the other three, or that at their meeting no reference to Ivan was made. Is it plausible that none of the three would mention the terrible shock they had after their discovery that Ivan was still alive? There is no evidence on this matter. The investigators did not record anything related to contacts among witnesses, and the matter was not thoroughly investigated in court.

Some doubts on this issue are justified because on other occasions the police investigators appeared to be unaware of such problems. The witnesses travelled together in the same aircraft to Fort Lauderdale, where the Fedorenko trial was held. They also stayed in the same hotel, had meals together, but were still supposed to make fully independent identifications. Boraks, who was not in full command of his memory when he was questioned in 1987, declared when asked about his journey to Fort Lauderdale, that he went there by train. Mrs. Radiwker, when asked how she travelled to Fort Lauderdale, replied: 'Not by train.' Thus she indicated, not only that she had followed the previous hearings, which she was not supposed to do, but also that she did not understand the importance of independence among witnesses.

The next successful witness was Josef Czarny, who was interviewed on September 21. At 1.00 p.m. he was interrogated about Fedorenko, at 2.15 p.m. about Demjanjuk. Two separate reports were prepared. Again the report on Fedorenko does not mention that Czarny recognized Demjanjuk. The second report, on Demjanjuk, says:

The witness is shown three brown cardboard pages with 17 photographs pasted on them. The witness points, at first sight, to photo 16, the photograph of Ivan Demjanjuk, and declares: 'This is Ivan, yes it is Ivan, the notorious Ivan. Thirty years have gone by, but I recognize him at first sight with complete certainty. I would know him, I believe, even in the dark. He was very tall, of sturdy frame, his face at the time was not as full and fat from gorging himself with food, as on the picture. However, it is the same face construction, the same nose, the same eyes and forehead, as he had at that time. A mistake is out of the question.'

Again we are faced with the problem of an initial non-identification of Demjanjuk in the statement of Fedorenko. In the 1987 Jerusalem hearing that point was raised by the defense.

Q. Mr. Czarny, you told us that on the 21st of September . . . when you were summoned to the Israel police in connection with pictures shown to you, when they showed you those pictures, you pointed to picture No. 16 and said 'This is Ivan the Terrible,' and a short while later you pointed to another picture and said that too is a Ukrainian familiar to you, is that true?

A. My first look was at Ivan. That's true. Ivan. Ivan. If it was 16, it was Ivan. It was the first look I saw.

Q. And you told the investigator that it was Ivan?

A. Yes.

Q. And then you went on to refer to someone else, whom you said you knew?

A. Yes. I said he is familiar to me, not that I know him, but he is familiar from Treblinka, very familiar.

Q. Are you quite sure that's how it happened?

A. To the best of my recollection.

Q. Look, I am telling you that the first time, when they showed you those pictures at the police, it was at 1.00 p.m. and you did in fact point to a picture, but it was not the picture of Ivan. You pointed to the picture of Fedorenko, picture No. 17. Ivan you did not point to at all. Not under any circumstances. You did not say here is Ivan of Treblinka. You did not say anything that has to do with Ivan. You pointed to picture No. 17 of Fedorenko.

A. What I remember, maybe it wasn't recorded, and I repeat what I said just a minute ago. At whatever stage it may have been, my first reflex was Ivan. If it was recorded or not, that I don't know. (JET, 1666)

A minute later Judge Levine intervened and presented the following clarification of what really happened:

The witness says that first he was shown the pictures and he identified the two pictures. First the picture of Ivan, and then the picture of the other one. After this process of identifying the pictures, they sat down and recorded his statements. One statement which refers to Fedorenko, and the second statement which refers to Ivan. The identification of the pictures, in keeping with his testimony was a procedure that was independent. Only later, after this procedure was over, was there the process of taking the deposition. (JET, 1675)

Judge Levine's reconstruction is elegant and very likely. But it stresses even more the fact that Mrs. Radiwker's written statements are sometimes made several hours after the event, and that they reconstruct the events in a more logical way than they occurred. We are asked to assume that there was, in fact, only one interview, which was reported as two interviews. But the decision to put certain facts in one of the other interviews would have been somewhat arbitrary, and there would always be a risk of confusing the two themes. Judge Levine's reconstruction does not explain what happened in the case of Turowski, because in the first statement he declared explicitly that he remembered only one name, Fedorenko. No other names. Also the problems with Rosenberg's testimony cannot be explained in this manner because Rosenberg was questioned twice, with a two-year interval. Another argument against Judge Levine's interpretation is that Czarny declared in the Fedorenko trial three times that he recognized only Fedorenko, no other person.

Czarny was all the time in camp 1, which means that the non-identification of other witnesses cannot be explained by the mere fact that they were only in camp 1.

If we disregard the problems in the recording procedure, we may accept the identification by Czarny as immediate and authentic. But the next witness, Schlomo Helman, caused a lot of uncertainty. He was interviewed by Mrs. Radiwker on September 29. Helman was in Treblinka from July 1942 till August 1943, longer than any other of the survivors. He was forced to assist in the construction of the gas chambers and remained all the time in camp 2. He worked alongside Ivan for many months, and was able to watch him from a few meters distance. Mrs. Radiwker's record says:

The name of Demjanjuk presented to me does not mean anything to me. When asked: Ivan was large, according to my recollection he could have been 30 years old. I do not remember any insignia. 'The witness was shown five photographs of Ukrainians, pasted on a brown cardboard. The witness cannot identify Ivan Demjanjuk. He points only at picture No. 17 (the photograph of Fedorenko) and declares: 'This man I have seen in Treblinka. The name Fedorenko presented to me is also unknown to me. I believe I have seen him in camp 1, but I have no further information about him.'

This failure must have come as a shock. Helman had a better opportunity than any other witness to observe Ivan. He recognized Fedorenko, which suggests that there was nothing wrong with his memory. He discussed Ivan before the identification attempt, hence he knew what he was looking for. Still he did not recognize Demjanjuk.

A puzzling aspect of this confrontation is that only five pictures were shown, not 17, as with Turowski, Goldfarb, Rosenberg, and Czarny; not eight as in the later cases of Boraks, Lindwasser, and Epstein, but a totally different page, containing only five pictures, the numbers 13–17. Why did the investigators compose a new spread? Did they not realize that a positive identification could have been rejected on chance considerations alone? The choice was really small for Helman: No. 15 was ostensibly Anton Rychalsky because his name was written on the picture; No. 17 he identified as Fedorenko; only 13, 14, and 16 remained. The fact that Helman still did not identify Demjanjuk suggests at least that the demand characteristics of the situation did not force him to guess. If this were to be generalized to the other witnesses, we could come to the conclusion that their positive identifications were also not the result of guessing. But if Helman resisted the urge to guess, we are still faced with the question why did he not identify Demjanjuk? Had he forgotten how Ivan looked? Had Demjanjuk, if he really was Ivan, changed too much in the course of the years? Or does it mean that Demjanjuk is not the same person as Ivan? The procedural errors made with previous witnesses weaken the impact of their identifications because the errors contributed to a positive response. But they strengthen Schlomo Helman's non-identification; despite the leading nature of the situation he did not perceive a resemblance between Demjanjuk's picture and the face of Ivan as he remembered it.

The cavalier manner in which non-identifications were discarded as unimportant illustrates how little understanding the investigators had of the logic of identification tests, shoddy as it is. If Turowski and Czarny declared that Demjanjuk's picture hit them in the face and caused a great shock, why did Helman not recognize him? We will never have an answer to this question, because Helman died before he could be questioned in court.

The next witness, Gustav Boraks, was questioned on September 30, 1976, first about Demjanjuk, then about Fedorenko. It is reasonable to assume, as with Czarny, that there was in fact only one interview, which resulted in two depositions. With respect to Demjanjuk the record says:

To a question: In connection with my work, I knew a Ukrainian of the camp staff, who was called Ivan Grozny. The name Demjanjuk means nothing to me. The witness is shown eight photographs of Ukrainian Nazi criminals, on a brown cardboard. The witness points at picture No. 16 (photograph of Ivan Demjanjuk) and declares: 'This is the likeness of Ivan Grozny. I recognize him with one hundred percent of certainty. I recognize him by his features. He was younger then, up to 25 years old, the face was not as full, but there is no doubt in my mind that he is the one.'

The identification sounds immediate and authentic. But the statement raises the question of why eight pictures were shown instead of the usual 17? Since Fedorenko could not serve as a foil, the effective lineup size was not more than seven. Apparently the investigators were not aware of the fact that a minimum of eight pictures is required by Israeli law. Or else they did not think the law was applicable to the investigation of Nazi crimes. Boraks was questioned in the Jerusalem court in 1987, but his memory failed him completely. His age was then 86.

On October 3, 1976, Mrs. Radiwker interviewed Abraham Lindwasser, again both on Demjanjuk and Fedorenko, in that order. His identification of Demjanjuk was immediate and positive. But now the identification of Fedorenko caused a problem. It says:

I recognize except Ivan Grozny, about whom I have already testified (Ivan Demjanjuk), also the man on picture 17. This man I know also by his name. His name is Fedorenko.

This time Mrs. Radiwker did not separate the two issues

completely. The identification of Demjanjuk is mentioned in the report on Fedorenko. Is this a slip? Or does it mean that Judge Levine's charitable reconstruction was incorrect, and that in other cases, where such references are missing, the other identification was not made? This problem is irrelevant in the case of Boraks because he was first interrogated about Demjanjuk. But for the others depositions about Fedorenko were made first. If Mrs. Radiwker had been consistent in the way she reported, the depositions about Fedorenko would have contained statements like: 'I recognize, besides Ivan Grozny. . .' But we know already that there are no statements of this sort.

EPSTEIN'S TESTIMONIES

Mrs. Radiwker transferred the case to her successor, Martin Kolar, in February 1978. Kolar questioned a new witness, Pinchas Epstein, on March 29, 1978. This was 18 months after Lindwasser was questioned. It is not known what happened in between, or why there was such a long delay, but the interval creates a problem because Epstein could have talked to many of the previous witnesses. He was asked by the defense about this in court.

Q. Is there a monument to those who died in Treblinka in the City of Tel Aviv, in the State of Israel?
A. A monument to the memory of those killed in Treblinka exists in the cemetery in Nahalat Yitzhak.
Q. Was there ever an occasion, Mr. Epstein, on which periodic gatherings take place of those who survived the Treblinka death camp?
A. Yes, on August 2nd we used to gather at the cemetery.
Q. Mr. Epstein, at the time you gather at the cemetery did you ever talk among yourselves?
A. When we gathered at the cemetery it is clear that we discussed things amongst ourselves.

Q. Mr. Epstein, are there any other occasions, for instance the time you might be visiting Yad Vashem or the Archives in Yad Vashem, where you might discuss your experience, for instance with Elijahu Rosenberg?
A. With Elijahu Rosenberg I meet on social occasions, weddings and similar pleasant occasions, and sometimes also at funerals and in private circles. (JET, 916)

Another fact that transpired from the cross-examination of Epstein is that Kolar did not warn witnesses that maybe there was no picture of any Treblinka guard in the photospread.

Q. Is it not true to say that before you were asked to identify photographs that it was explained to you that possibly there was a picture of Ivan and possibly there was not?
A. No, I wasn't told whether it was possible or not possible. (JET, 927)

A further matter emerging from the cross-examination is that a verbal description of Ivan was available long before the first photospread was composed. It should, in principle, have been possible to compose a fair photospread on the basis of this information.

Q. Can you give the description, as you gave it already in 1961?
A. As I remember him, yes, a tall, thickset, shortnecked – age as I said earlier between 22 and 25. (JET, 698)

Epstein identified both Demjanjuk and Fedorenko.

The witness was then shown a photo album: a brown cardboard strip with eight photos numbered 10 to 17. The witness pointed out photo No. 16 and said: 'This photo reminds me very strongly of Ivan.
The photo is not quite clear and also the change in age must make a difference. The shape of the face, especially the rounded forehead, strengthens my feeling that it is Ivan. The characteristic short neck on broad shoulders – that's exactly what Ivan looked like. I recognize photo No. 17 as that of Fedorenko.'

The surprising aspect of this statement is that Kolar now mentions both identifications in one deposition, whereas two weeks later he failed to mention that Rosenberg identified Demjanjuk when asked about Fedorenko.

Epstein's identification was quite positive; the obvious problem is his frequent contact with Rosenberg. The last witness, Rajchman, raises the same type of problem. He was interviewed for the first time on March 12, 1980, but since this interview involved a totally different set of pictures, the discussion of Rajchman's testimony will be postponed.

Epstein's testimony concluded the confrontation of 15

witnesses with Demjanjuk's 1951 immigration portrait. Seven of these identified him, but the identifications are not indisputable. Much dispute is caused by the investigators' reporting, which makes it impossible to know fully what really happened, and what was really said by the witnesses.

CONFRONTATIONS WITH THE TRAWNIKI PICTURE

On December 17, 1979, almost two years after Kolar had succeeded Mrs. Radiwker, a letter was received from the Office of Special Investigations (OSI) in the United States, which had taken over the responsibility for the Demjanjuk case. The letter asked the Israelis to confront witnesses with a new set of photographs, to which I will refer as the Trawniki spread. The procedures used for these confrontations were described by Mr. Kolar in his testimony.

The Trawniki spread consisted of eight pictures showing men in military uniforms. One picture, which allegedly is a portrait of John Demjanjuk in the year 1942, was taken from the so-called Trawniki document. This is the card that was released by the government of the Soviet Union, and which was used to prove that Demjanjuk was trained in Trawniki, the place where Ukrainians were prepared for service in concentration and death camps. The authenticity of the Trawniki document is disputed by the defense, and it is not certain whether the Trawniki picture is really a portrait of Demjanjuk. The special value of the Trawniki picture is that it would show Demjanjuk at the correct age, and not ten years after his alleged presence in Treblinka. For the sake of argument I will assume that the Trawniki picture may be an authentic portrait of Demjanjuk, even if the Trawniki document should prove to be a forgery. A failure to recognize the Trawniki picture would be highly informative because now it could not be attributed to a difference with respect to age. The only reasons for not recognizing the Trawniki picture could be that this is not a picture of Demjanjuk, or that Demjanjuk was not in Treblinka, or that the witnesses did not remember. Any of the three explanations cause serious problems for the prosecution. Hence the showing of the Trawniki picture was a risky attempt to check the memory of witnesses who had already positively identified Demjanjuk, and the investigating team should be praised for accepting this risk.

The Trawniki spread consisted of eight pictures, the picture from the Trawniki document and seven other pictures of people suspected of Nazi crimes. It is not clear on what basis the foils were selected. The photographs were of a better quality, and better standardized than the album spread. The faces were of about the same size. There were also some obvious differences: the eight people wore different uniforms, some with insignia Ivan could never have worn; two of the people were looking straight into the camera, including the man from the Trawniki document. Demjanjuk is the only blond person in the set, see Figure 4.2.

The pictures were not pasted on a sheet of cardboard, but were presented as a pile of eight separate pictures. The first witness, Epstein, was given the pictures in a pile, for the others the pictures were spread out by the investigator. It is not known in which order the pictures were in the pile, or how they were arranged when they were spread out. The OSI letter instructed the investigator to turn over pictures recognized by the witnesses, and to request the witnesses to place their signatures at the back of those pictures.

The first witness who was confronted with the Trawniki spread was Pinchas Epstein, on December 25, 1979, at 11.00 a.m. Epstein went through the pictures and when he came to the target picture, he said (in Kolar's words): 'This is how I remember him. This is what he looked like.'

But he recognized also another picture, which he said represented Nicolai, the other person in charge of the diesel engine. This second identification was incorrect, because the picture was of Schmidt, who was never in Treblinka. Kolar did not request Epstein to sign this picture, because 'It was not an unequivocal identification'. In fact Epstein had said: 'This face reminds me of the likeness of Nicolai.' It is probably alright to classify such uncertain identifications as non-identifications, but it should be remembered that Epstein used exactly the same words when he identified

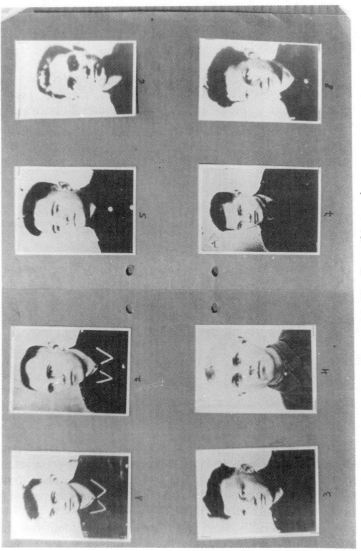

Figure 4.2: The Trawniki spread.

Demjanjuk in 1978. The free decision of an investigator to accept or reject an uncertain identification introduces an undesirable degree of arbitrariness.

The second witness, Rosenberg, was interviewed on the same day at 1.30 p.m. One question which arose was of course whether Epstein and Rosenberg met between the sessions. Kolar said they did not:

A. My working day officially was eight hours. Unofficially it extended well beyond that. Mr. Rosenberg and Mr. Epstein came to me at times with a vast interval in between. . .
Q. Did you ask Mr. Rosenberg whether he had met Epstein? Or did you ask Epstein whether he had come up against Rosenberg?
A. No, I had summoned them at such times that they could not possibly have known each other's coming. (JET, 3282)

It is not clear why Kolar is so certain that there was no possibility. The interval was not that long, probably in the order of an hour. The investigators received Epstein's name from Rosenberg. The two were in fact closely befriended, and Kolar knew about this. In his own words:

In the hotel they showed me pictures of weddings of their children, and I saw that at the wedding of Levkowitch, or rather of Rosenberg – Levkowitch was there, and Epstein was there too. At Epstein's weddings, the others were there too. And from this I inferred that there is a warm friendship between them. (JET, 3137)

If this is true the real question is not whether the interval was long enough to keep Epstein and Rosenberg separated, but whether it was long enough to allow contacts. Could they not have met for lunch together? Kolar seems to be totally unaware of this problem.

Rosenberg took about two minutes to identify the Trawniki picture. He said:

This reminds me very much of Ivan, but I think that this is a photograph taken in a period before Treblinka. I saw him fuller in the face. Maybe by then he managed to eat better.

Rosenberg pointed also at two other people, but his signature was only put on the back of the Trawniki picture, which contained Epstein's signature already. This means that by now Rosenberg knew that Epstein had picked the same picture. Kolar must have assumed that also after this session Epstein, Rosenberg and Levkowitch did not discuss the case because the next witness, Sonia Levkowitch, was allowed to testify two days later. Although she identified the Trawniki picture, she was not presented as a witness in the Jerusalem court.

A crucial role is played by the witness Chil Meir Rajchman. He was interviewed by people from the OSI in a hotel room in New York, on March 12, 1980. The investigation was conducted by Mr. Fusi. Two other investigators, Moscowitz and Parker, were also present. The most amazing fact about this interview is that Fusi's report which was presented to the court was written on February 13, 1987, seven years after it took place. No transcript of the actual interview was entered as evidence. This means that not only Rajchman's testimony is impeded by a long retention period, but also Fusi's report of it.

One riddle in Fusi's report is that it states clearly that the interview was conducted in the English language, without an interpreter. This is impossible, as Rajchman does not speak or understand English. His languages are Yiddish and Spanish, not even Hebrew. If Fusi does not remember the interpreter, how can we be assured that all other details are reported correctly?

Fusi lost the unique opportunity of confronting a witness with the Trawniki picture before having seen the 1951 album picture. Instead of first showing the Trawniki spread he showed a new set, composed of the 1951 album picture and seven other pictures. The seven foils came from immigration files in the possession of OSI. Fusi declared that the photo-spread was prepared such that none of the photos would appear to be suggestive. Without any preparatory questioning Fusi put the stack of eight pictures before Rajchman, face down. The instruction was to turn over the photographs, to examine each of them carefully, and to see whether he could identify anyone. Rajchman was told that it was possible that none of the photographs were those of

Treblinka guards. The inspection time was several minutes according to Fusi, though more than that according to Rajchman. Rajchman identified Demjanjuk's picture. In court Rajchman mentioned even an inspection time of three hours. According to Fusi's report Rajchman was fairly certain that this was Ivan, and he signed the picture at the back.

Subsequently Fusi conferred in private with the two other investigators and decided to show Rajchman the Trawniki spread as well. How exactly the spread was composed is not clear. Fusi stated:

Although that photospread consisted of the same eight photos as those contained in Photospread A8 237 417–q, I do not believe Mr. Rajchman was shown that exact photospread.

This statement presents a difficult puzzle: Rajchman was shown the same photos as were in the Trawniki spread (which is indeed known as A8 237 417–q), but for some reason it was still not the same spread. What was the difference then? Why should a court accept an identification test if the composition of the spread is not even known?

Whatever the answer may be, the relevant fact is that Rajchman did not recognize the Trawniki portrait. The same spread was shown to him during the Cleveland trial in 1981. Now he recognized the Trawniki picture. In the 1987 Jerusalem testimony he said about this:

A. There I recognized a picture that was even more similar than the other one, because in court they showed me a picture which was just the right weight, even more similar to the way he looks in Treblinka.

Q. They showed you a picture that you signed? Did they show you that one as well, the picture you signed in New York?

A. Maybe, but in the picture which they showed in New York he was wearing a tie, and in Treblinka he wore a uniform, so that it was easier for me to recognize his face. (JET, 2214)

Here Rajchman gives the impression that he saw only one spread in the hotel room in New York, while the second set was shown to him for the first time in Cleveland. But this is not at all how it was reported by Fusi. Rajchman himself did not remember the showing of the second spread in New York:

I was shown a packet of pictures. I don't know whether there was one set or two sets. In any event, it took me a long time. (JET, 2338)

Defense counsel was not satisfied with this statement and asked:

In the court in the United States you identified this picture as the picture of Ivan, and you also said that it is easy for you to identify this picture because the man in this picture is in uniform. . . The investigator, the interrogators in the United States say that in 1980, when you were at the hotel with them, they showed you that very same picture, not alone but among other pictures. After you had identified the picture which you told us about as having been the one of Ivan and you looked at this picture . . . and at the others and you did not identify any picture, neither this one nor any of the others as being familiar at all. How do you account for this? If you say that it is so easy for you to identify the picture because of the uniform? (JET, 2340)

Rajchman could not solve the problem, probably because he did not remember the presentation of the Trawniki spread in the New York hotel. His helpless reply was:

I can't say. One thing I can say which is that the lawyer is not speaking the truth when he says that I talked English. (JET, 2342)

The last witness who was asked to identify Demjanjuk in the Trawniki spread was again Gustav Boraks, on February 3, 1981. At that time Boraks was eighty, and the Israeli investigators wanted only to test whether he was still fit enough to give testimony in Cleveland. First he was shown the Trawniki spread, then the album spread. He identified the Trawniki picture and Demjanjuk's album picture. There is no official report of this session but only an unsigned memorandum. This procedure is of course wholly unacceptable because the suggestion is created that Boraks was prepared for pointing at the correct pictures in the Cleveland court. Only the presence of a defense counsel could have prevented this.

In 1988 it became apparent that identification attempts had been made with at least 24 more witnesses. Fifteen of these witnesses had seen Ivan long enough to make a positive identification. These attempts were never before available to the defense, although none of them was successful. I will return to this aspect of the case in Chapter 5.

IN-COURT IDENTIFICATIONS

Five witnesses testified for the prosecution in 1987 in the Jerusalem court: Rosenberg, Czarny, Boraks, Epstein, and Rajchman. Turowski, Goldfarb, and Lindwasser had died before that time, and Levkowitch withdrew her testimony. The five witnesses were asked to look at the photographs during the court session. All of them identified Demjanjuk with absolute certainty. They were also asked to identify Demjanjuk as he was sitting in the dock. All five succeeded at this task and pronounced one hundred percent certainty.

Although these identifications raised a tremendous amount of public emotion, I will not further consider them as serious evidence because it is obvious that by now the witnesses had seen an incalculable number of pictures of Demjanjuk on television and in newspapers.

Table 4.3: An overview of 13 positive out-of-court identifications

Date	Name	Spread	Identification	Problems
9 May 76	Abraham Goldfarb	17 album pictures	I believe I recognize.	Did not recognize in first session.
10 May 76	Eugen Turowski	17 album pictures	I recognize with full assurance.	Did not recognize the day before. Says he knew name.
11 May 76	Elijahu Rosenberg	17 album pictures	I see a great resemblance. I decline to identify with certainty.	Testified that Ivan is dead. Did not recognize in 1978. Contacts?
21 Sept 76	Josef Czarny	17 album pictures	This is Ivan.	Did not recognize in first session. Contacts?

30 Sept 76	Gustav Boraks	8 album pictures	I recognize with 100% certainty.	Contacts?
3 Oct 76	Abraham Lindwasser	8 album pictures	I recognize him with full certainty.	Contacts?
29 Mar 78	Pinchas Epstein	8 album pictures	Reminds me strongly of Ivan.	Contacts?
25 Dec 79	Pinchas Epstein	8 Trawniki pictures	This is how I remember him.	Misidentified Nikolai.
25 Dec 79	Elijahu Rosenberg	8 Trawniki pictures	Reminds me very much.	Contacts?
27 Dec 79	Sonia Levkowitch	8 Trawniki pictures	Positive.	Contacts? No testimony in court.
3 Feb 80	Gustav Boraks	8 album pictures. 8 Trawniki pictures.	Positive in both cases.	No official report. Third presentation of album pictures.
12 Mar 80	Chil Meir Rajchman	8 OSI pictures	Fairly certain.	Report 7 years later. Failed on Trawniki spread.

CONCLUSION

Altogether nine different witnesses produced 13 positive out-of-court identifications, which are all presented in Table 4.3. Few of these identifications were without problems. Some of them are even highly questionable. On the other hand there were an unknown number of failed identifications; probably eight by witnesses interrogated by the Israeli police; 24 by witnesses questioned by the OSI; and possibly, depending upon the literal or free interpretation of the official documents, another five by Turowski, Goldfarb, Rosenberg, Czarny, and Rajchman.

5 Violations of Rules in Demjanjuk's Identification

The procedures used for the identification of John Demjanjuk as Ivan the Terrible were not without problems. They will be listed in this chapter. Following the distinction made in the last section of Chapter 2, it is possible to discuss two groups of variables that influence the reliability of identifications by eyewitnesses. The first group is related to estimator variables: those that are essential features of the case, and that are not under the control of the investigators. Examples are the exposure time during the crime, the violent nature of the crime, and the length of the retention period. Although it is my strong conviction that such variables were extremely important, and that the court sitting in judgment on Demjanjuk should have considered them carefully, I will refrain from discussing estimator variables here. The reason is that there is little scientific information about the effects of estimator variables in the case of death camp survivors. This does not mean that courts should disregard these variables; but they will have to form their own judgment, unassisted by scientific research.

System variables also influence the reliability of identifications: they are related to the identification procedures and are under the control of the investigators. The rules presented in Chapter 3 have to do with system variables only. The present chapter will discuss whether or not these rules could have been applied in the case of John Demjanjuk, and whether they were applied.

THE INVESTIGATORS

Most of the investigations were directed by Mrs. Radiwker and Mr. Kolar, both employed by the Division for the Investigation of Nazi Crimes, attached to the Israeli police. Rule 22 specifies that appropriate training should be given to police officers in charge of identification procedures because identification is, in most cases, tricky and crucial. There is no written law that requires special training, but the defense can at least request that identification tests are administered in a professional manner. Did the Israeli authorities ensure that their investigators were professionally competent?

Mrs. Radiwker was born in 1906. She was trained as a lawyer at the University of Krakow, and graduated in 1930. Subsequently she practiced law in Poland and the Soviet Union, with an interruption during the war. In 1964 she emigrated to Israel, where after a few months she was hired by the police. She remained active till 1978, when she retired at the age of 72. A lawyer does not automatically qualify for police work. Accordingly, Mrs. Radiwker was asked in cross-examination about her training as a police investigator.

Q. Madame, can you indicate whether or not when you were accepted into the unit to investigate National Socialist crimes, or Nazi crimes – here in Israel – did you receive any special training for your work?
A. I did not receive – I was not accepted on the basis of any special socialist activity. I was accepted to conduct an investigation concerning Nazi war crimes.
Judge Levine: In this connection, did you receive some sort of special training?
A. No. (JET, 2725)

And later:

Q. Can you indicate, madame, based upon my prior question, did you receive any training in investigative work or anti-fascist investigation or Nazi investigation – during the time shortly after you were accepted into this special unit to investigate Nazi crimes?
A. I began working, working. I began working. I read judgments of the Germans. I worked, but I did it myself. (JET, 2727)

Later Judge Levine explained that she did not take any sort of course or training. The effects of her not being trained are evident throughout the whole procedure, and I will also refer to them in later sections. Here are some small excerpts of the cross-examination, illustrating the nature of the problems.

Q. The name Fedorenko, did you mention the name Fedorenko explicitly? It says so here. . . Let me read it to you. 'To the question whether the person in picture No. 17 who is supposed to be Fedorenko, he said I can't identify him'. So you mentioned Fedorenko.
A. I don't see anything wrong with that as an investigator. (JET, 2872)

In fact she does not think it is wrong to direct the witness' attention to one specific picture, which is a very leading procedure.

Q. You showed photo No. 16 together with 7 additional photos out of which those which were not blurred, and there are almost none of those, that one of the few things that were not blurred on the photos was the hair, and Ivan's head is almost, is almost bald and very high forehead. And the other 6 photos are the photos of people with plenty of black hair. Why did you do this? Why didn't you arrange it in a different way?
A. I simply put before them what I had received. I am really not responsible for Demjanjuk's bald pate.
Q. That is obvious. But you are responsible for the identification. (JET, 2894)

In fact Mrs. Radiwker saw nothing wrong in presenting a photospread containing foils that did not fit the description of Ivan.

Q. Madame, do you know how many pictures is the minimum that must be shown to a witness when you ask the witness to identify pictures?
A. According to the guidelines as I've already said, at least 3 pictures.
Q. No, I'm not asking about that.
Judge Levine: He's asking now about general lineups, usually, when you do it at the initiative of the Israeli police.
A. I work according to whoever asks for it . . . the Germans or the Americans. The Germans ask for few pictures, more or less eight as a maximum.
Q. In Israel, do you know what the requirement is?
A. I don't deal with – I do not practice law now. I know that the police

abides by the conventional procedure. Whatever is accepted by the courts in this country. But I simply don't have occasion to deal with this. I've dealt with matters that concern the Germans and the Americans. And as you see here, there are at least 3 pictures here. And the Germans also sent very few.

Q. I haven't received an answer, with all due respect. How many pictures in Israel does a person have to have for a lineup to be valid? (JET, 2898)

The fact is that Mrs. Radiwker did not know that in Israel a photospread should contain eight pictures.

Martin Kolar was born in 1920 in Czechoslovakia. He did not receive any legal training, but had some experience with investigating Nazi crimes in the years 1945–47. He came to Israel in 1965 and was hired by the Division for the Investigation of Nazi Crimes almost instantly. In February 1978 he had over 12 years of experience with this type of work, but he did not know all rules for identification procedures. In Israel it is required by law that defense counsel is present at lineup procedures. Kolar was asked about this in the cross examination.

Q. Now tell me, first of all had you heard about this fact that the defense counsel would have to be present at an identification lineup, have you ever heard such a thing? ———
A. I did not know nor did the superior know about this. It was not customary ever. Here I fulfilled to the letter what I was asked to do by the Attorney General in Washington and this is what we did. . .
Q. Did you say earlier that you don't know?
A. That's right.
Q. Now, do you know?
A. Yes, come to think of it.
Q. Do I understand correctly that only at this very moment at this trial you found out, following my question and following the question of the Honorable Bench, that there has to be a defense counsel present at a lineup? (JET, 3252)

The counsel's bewilderment is justified: nobody had ever told Kolar that this was required by Israeli law.

Another issue is the instruction concerning the fact that perhaps the photo of the wanted person is not in the lineup. Israeli regulations require that this possibility is explicitly mentioned to witnesses before they attempt an identification.

> Q. Now, you have heard that the witness should not be told 'Tell me if you recognize someone', but rather 'The person that you know, he may be in the pictures, but maybe he is not in the pictures'.
> A. Let me correct myself. I said to him, 'Look and see if there is someone you know.' I didn't say that the person may not be there.
> Q. I know you didn't say that. I am asking something else. I am asking whether you ever heard that this coda should be added. I know you didn't do so.
> A. I have heard more or less in the month when I conducted that questioning; it was about then that I heard about it.
> Judge Levine: Excuse me?
> A. It was something new for me, this formula. (JET, 3258)

Another question is the photographing of the Trawniki spread and the way they were presented to the witnesses. There was a directive that requires photographs to be taken by the photography department of the investigation unit.

> Judge Levine: Mr. Sheftel's question, as far as I understood it, why didn't you deem it necessary to document the event or the occasion of indicating the photographs in 1979 by way of a photograph; and for that purpose one can summon a photographer from the Unit, so that he can come and carry out this function?
> A. It was not customary.
> Q. At your unit?
> A. It was simply not customary.
> Q. Did you know about this directive? That it was advisable?
> A. No. (JET, 3292)

The lack of awareness of the rules for identifications is remarkable, given that Demjanjuk was investigated by Israeli officials for a legal procedure that would end in an Israeli court. But the reality is that throughout the whole procedure the investigators were under the impression that they were investigating for the American INS and OSI, probably as a preparation for a trial in the United States. Therefore they were simply following instructions sent to them from the US, without ever questioning them. Nor does it seem to me based on my review of the Walus, Fedorenko, and Demjanjuk cases that the Americans knew how identification should be conducted. It can be concluded that the Israeli investigators could not be blamed for the mistakes of others. But it cannot be denied that all identifications in the Demjanjuk case were conducted by officers who received an insufficient amount of training. The many procedural mistakes summarized in the next sections are a consequence of this lack of training.

THE PHOTOSPREADS

Mugfile or lineup
The photospread used for the first identification of John Demjanjuk as Ivan the Terrible was the album spread, consisting exclusively of pictures of Ukrainians living in the US and suspected of Nazi crimes. This spread was a mugfile, and not a photographic lineup. This can be concluded from the following facts.

- All pictures were of possible suspects, there were no innocent foils. The witnesses could not be caught out making an error. Each response would have initiated further investigations. The fact that Demjanjuk was accused on the basis of testimony by survivors of Treblinka, although the investigators were convinced he was in Sobibor, is the best illustration of this situation.
- There was no attempt to match the pictures in the spread with descriptions of the wanted criminal, produced prior to the test. In fact there were no such descriptions.
- There was no attempt to remove details that might betray the identity of some of the people in the spread.

The only purpose of mugfile selection is to obtain the names of possible suspects. Once those names are known the proof of identity should be obtained through proper identification tests. In the case of Demjanjuk the mugfile selection proved to be fruitful. He was recognized by witnesses in a quite unexpected way, since he was never previously suspected of Nazi activities in Treblinka. But once he was recognized by Turowski and Goldfarb, there was no reason to continue with mugfiles till the end, using up all the available witnesses. The correct procedure would have been to take the descriptions produced by Turowski and Goldfarb, and to select foils, at least seven according to Israeli law, that fitted these descriptions: 'A full round face' (Goldfarb) 'A round full face, a short neck, a high forehead with a bald pate starting' (Turowski). The later subjects were all summoned specifically to identify Demjanjuk; there was no reason to confound this case with the investigation of Fedorenko. The Trawniki spread shown to four witnesses and the OSI spread shown to Rajchman were also not proper photographic lineups. Hence, in my opinion, no witness was ever tested in a proper identification procedure, because Rule 4 was violated.

Effective size
Obviously the investigators and the courts in Cleveland and Jerusalem were of the opinion that mugfiles can be used for identification purposes, and that the spreads were proper lineups. Therefore it would be useful to judge the value of the spreads as photographic lineups. The procedure proposed by Doob and Kirschenbaum (1973) is to present a verbal description to mock witnesses, and then to ask them whether they can identify the suspect in the lineup. I followed this procedure with 25 mock witnesses. They were given the following instruction: 'We are looking for a man with a full round face, a short wide neck, a bald pate starting. We will give you a set of eight photographs; please point to the person who is most likely to be the wanted person.' Then they were shown the third album page, with photographs 10 to 17 on it. The reason why only eight album pictures were shown instead of 17 is that three of the five witnesses who testified in the Jerusalem court saw eight pictures, whereas Boraks concentrated on page three because he was asked to identify Fedorenko. Rosenberg was first presented with 17 photographs. All 25 mock witnesses pointed to picture No. 16 of John Demjanjuk, without any exception. All mock witnesses declared that they had no suspicion that the test was related to the Demjanjuk trial, and that they had never seen a picture of Demjanjuk before. Thus, given the information that the wanted person has a

round face, a short neck, starting to go bald, it is 100 percent possible to guess that Demjanjuk is the target. This does not mean that the real witnesses did not recognize Demjanjuk, it only means that the photospread was not a fair lineup. The effective lineup size was only 1.0. That is, the lineup was no better than a showup, there was only one plausible candidate. It is clear that the minimal effective size was brought about by the neglect of the differences between a mugfile and a photographic lineup. The mistake was first made by the American INS, but was not corrected by the Israeli investigators. Talking about the Fedorenko investigation, Mrs. Radiwker said the following about this.

Q. Tell me please, why did you put before all the witnesses photos of which you yourself say there is no resemblance whatsoever with Fedorenko, much less any resemblance with photo No. 16?

A. I've already stated that we had very explicit guidelines issued by the American authorities. An American authority was the authority which requested certain proceedings and we simply fulfilled their request. We had to abide by the guidelines and it said explicitly to the extent possible, photos resembling the person to be identified, I think I have replied to your question. (JET, 2892)

Thus the American instructions did at least allude to the choice of plausible foils, within the set of 43 album pictures. But even that was not attempted, because the pictures were all glued onto cardboard.

A closer inspection of page three of the album spread makes it abundantly clear why it was so easy to guess that Demjanjuk is the suspect. The foils were not chosen on the basis of descriptions produced prior to the identifications. In fact there was no attempt to get such descriptions. The memories of the witnesses were tested through the photographs, not through interrogation. The result is that none of the foils bore any resemblance to Demjanjuk. His portrait was the only one that could be described as round face, short neck, balding. Some of the faces were notably non-round, non-balding. Demjanjuk's face on the picture was much larger than any other face. Two of the others were logically excluded: Fedorenko because he had been identified previously by most witnesses and could have been familiar to all witnesses; Rychalsky because in some tests his name was on his picture.

A fair photographic lineup could have been arranged without too much effort. It took me about one afternoon to come up with photographs of seven round-faced, short-necked, balding males of the right age. The 1951 Immigration picture of Demjanjuk was added to these seven, in order to form a new and possibly better photographic lineup. This spread was shown to 25 mock witnesses, students at Leiden University. They were given a description of Ivan and asked to select his picture. Only two of them pointed at Demjanjuk's picture.

A slightly different demonstration of suggestion in the photographic lineup was presented by Douglas Detterman, a psychologist who prepared a memorandum for the Cleveland trial. He showed the OSI spread (containing the 1951 Immigration picture) and the Trawniki spread to 58 students at Case Western Reserve University. He did not describe Ivan to these mock witnesses, but only asked them to point at the most guilty looking person in the spreads. Sixteen of the subjects pointed at Demjanjuk's picture in the OSI spread; eighteen pointed at the Trawniki picture in the Trawniki spread. Thus even without any description of the target, about 30 percent of the witnesses would identify the target if they were only searching for the most guilty looking person. Again this type of suggestion could have been avoided. The lineup composed in my institute was offered to 25 subjects who were asked to identify the most guilty looking participant. Only two students pointed to Demjanjuk's picture (Detterman, 1981)

REPEATED TESTING

Rule 7 specifies that witnesses should be asked to identify the suspect only once because in subsequent attempts it would be possible to rely on the image remembered from previous identifications. This rule applies to all identifications with the Trawniki spread that were presented in court. Epstein, Rosenberg, Rajchman and Boraks had all seen the 1951 Immigration picture before they saw the Trawniki picture.

The Trawniki spread was considerably biased against Demjanjuk because again there were no foils that fitted with a rough description of him. Some foils wore uniforms and insignia that Demjanjuk never had. Although the defense denied that the Trawniki picture is actually a representation of Demjanjuk, it cannot be denied that there is a certain likeness. How difficult would it be for mock witnesses to identify the Trawniki picture after having seen the 1951 Immigration portrait? The 25 mock witnesses to whom I showed the album spread, and who were all successful at identifying Demjanjuk, were subsequently shown the Trawniki spread. The question put to them was: 'Do you see the same person in this spread?' I took away the album pictures, so that they had to rely on memory only. Sixteen mock witnesses were successful at this task, which means that, once you know the immigration portrait, it is not too difficult to identify the target in the Trawniki spread. Thus a successful identification of the Trawniki picture does not prove much, because the witnesses could easily rely on the album spread they had seen before. And that is exactly the reason why repeated testing should be avoided.

The prosecution in Jerusalem spent much effort in proving that the immigration picture and the Trawniki picture represented the same person. They even claimed that this is obvious to anyone who takes a good look. But then it is even more surprising that they decided to show both pictures to the same witnesses. My small experimental comparison reveals that the resemblance between the two pictures is, in fact, not so large: 36 percent of the mock witnesses pointed to another participant in the Trawniki spread.

Repeated testing, but with a reversal of the order of presentation, first the Trawniki spread, and then the Immigration picture, would not have been any better. Detterman tried this order. He presented the Trawniki portrait to his subjects, and asked them to identify the same person in the OSI spread. Fifty-eight percent of the subjects were successful at this task.

These results show that even if the Trawniki spread had been less biased against the suspect, the results obtained with this spread were unacceptable because of the repeated character of the identification attempts.

RECORDING AND REPORTING

Complete records
It was already explained that Mrs. Radiwker and Mr. Kolar wrote reports to the American authorities after the actual identification procedures were concluded. It is also clear from the previous chapter that these reports did not present a full account of what had happened, at the very least. The matter of accurate reporting came up several times in the Jerusalem court. Of course both Mrs. Radiwker and Mr. Kolar claimed that their reporting was always accurate and complete. Here is an example of such a discussion. The issue is the numbering of photographs in the album spread.

Judge Levine: Were they marked, were they numbered?
A. From 1 to 17.
Judge Levine: In sequence?
A. Yes those were the first three (pages).
Q. Do you remember this despite the fact that it does not appear in writing in Goldfarb's deposition, for example?
A. The decision of what to write in a transcript or a deposition is up to me. After all I keep the record and the record must include everything that happened. And everything that did happen does appear there. And I don't have to go beyond that.
Q. Why then, in Turowski's record, doesn't it say that when you showed him the picture he got excited and said 'Ivan, Ivan,' and how things happened, and so on, if everything has to appear in the record?
A. What is important. . .
Q. You decided.
A. What counts is that the record must say that he identified him at first sight. For me that was what was important. (JET, 2864)

Mrs. Radiwker is obviously mistaken here. The record must reflect much more than whom the witness identified. A properly structured report should describe the preparation of the lineup, the participants or the pictures of the participants, the descriptions of the criminal produced by the witness prior to the test, the instruction to the witness, the choice made by the witness and any information volunteered during the choice process, the time log of the procedure, and finally all relevant facts that may be needed to interpret correctly the identification, or the failure thereof. In this latter category there would be a record of previous identification attempts by the same witness, contacts with other witnesses, information received from other sources, and a justification of all instances in which a breach of the rules occurred. The reports of Mrs. Radiwker do not even come close to this requirement. Here is an example, the report written after the identification by Gustav Boraks.

To a question. In connection with my work I knew a Ukrainian of the camp staff, who was called Ivan Grozny. The name Demjanjuk means nothing to me. The witness is shown 8 photographs of Ukrainian Nazi criminals, on a brown cardboard. The witness points at picture No. 16 (photograph of Ivan Demjanjuk) and declares: This is the likeness of Ivan Grozny. I recognize him with one hundred percent of certainty. I recognize him by his features. He was younger then, up to 25 years old, the face was not as full, but there is no doubt in my mind that he is the one. . . Ivan wore a black uniform and on his cap he wore the deathhead (skull) emblem.

The whole procedure is summarized in one sentence: 'The witness is shown eight photographs of Ukrainian Nazi criminals, on a brown cardboard.' We have to rely on Mrs. Radiwker's memory to find out which eight photographs, what instruction was given, how long Boraks needed.

Tape recording
It should have been clear from the beginning that the Demjanjuk investigation, like all other cases against Nazi criminals from Treblinka, would attract international interest. Even when the written procedures did not request accurate recording, still the investigating authority should have understood that their work would be evaluated according to international criteria. The hearings of the Jerusalem court were shown on television all over the world. A continuous daily coverage was given in Israel from February 1987 till February 1988. But the investigators were deprived of the most primitive technical facilities. They had no steno-

graphers who could make a full transcript of the interrogations. There was not even a simple tape recorder to record the interviews. Defense counsel asked Mrs. Radiwker about this.

Q. Mrs. Radiwker, can you tell me from our discussion this morning, or your examination before the court this morning, with regard to the issue of the taking of testimony from witnesses, can you tell me why, when you took the testimony from the survivor witnesses involved in the investigation of Fedorenko, in the investigation of John Demjanjuk, why when you took these things down, they were not taken down by means of an electronic device such as a tape recorder?
A. We weren't so sophisticated yet.
Q. In other words, madam, what you are saying is that in 1976 the level of sophistication of the investigative unit that you served with had not reached the level of using a tape recorder, is that right, madam?
A. Yes, we just didn't use it, we didn't have such things. (JET, 2777)

Also Mr. Kolar was interviewed about this issue.

Q. In 1978 when tape recorders were readily available and fairly inexpensive, sir, why was it in taking all of these testimonies . . . why weren't these recorded sir, for purposes not only of your own reference within the file, but certainly in terms of reference many years later, such as today when we are trying to recall from memory your notes, those things that you consider to be essential. Why wasn't it tape-recorded sir?
A. How unfortunate that you did never visit our unit and make that proposal at the time, and did not tell us where to get the wherewithall, the budget that we didn't have available. . .
Judge Levine: For your information, sir, even today still neither the Israeli police nor the courts in Israel have the privilege or the good fortune of using such sophisticated and obvious and taken for granted devices considering the budgets available to the United States over there. That is how it is over here and the witness was very surprised by your question for this reason, but he answered you sincerely. (JET, 3228)

Although Judge Levine is essentially right, he misses the point entirely. The question is not whether the Israeli police could afford a tape recorder, but whether a court should accept evidence that leaves so many questions unanswered while these questions would have been answered by the investment of a few dollars. The investigation of Fedorenko and Demjanjuk was requested by the American INS and later the OSI. These authorities paid for the travel and the expenses of numerous witnesses in the trials against both suspects. Of course they could have supplied a tape recorder, if such a request had been received. But I can only conclude that no one, either in the United States, or in Israel, felt a need for a reliable recording of testimony. The discussions that arose in court prove how wrong they were. The question is now whether a suspect should run the risk of becoming the victim of this shortsightedness?

I will give one example of a crucial question that would have been resolved by a full record. The question concerns the identification by Goldfarb, the first identification of Ivan that was ever made, if we are to believe the official documents. The question posed by the defense counsel is whether the name of Ivan was first mentioned by Goldfarb, or first by Mrs. Radiwker. It may be remembered that Goldfarb said, in his testimony on Fedorenko, that the man in picture No. 16 'Looked familiar'. What happened in the second testimony?

Q. Now look, an hour and a half later, you questioned him again?
A. Yes.
Q. And this time he says, as you said it in German, he uses the name Ivan. In other words he refers to picture No. 16, he says what he says about the nature of the identification, and he uses the name Ivan. Now all of this happened, did you ask him anything specific about Ivan before he said that? Did you mention the name Ivan?
———
Judge Dorner: Did *you* mention the name Ivan or was it Mr. Goldfarb who mentioned the name Ivan of his own accord, that is the question to the best of my understanding.
A. I don't think he mentioned of his own accord. I asked him if he recognizes or identifies Ukrainians who were on the staff. I [took] a deposition, like any deposition, and it was then that he said, 'And I think I remember him'.
Judge Levine: Yes, but the question is this. When he said that the person appearing in picture No. 16 is familiar to him, did he say who this person was? Did he mention the name of that person?
A. No. No.
Q. When you took the testimony from him, concerning Demjanjuk, did you use the name Ivan before he referred to the picture?
A. No. I don't remember. I don't remember. I wrote down the description like I always did. (JET, 2871)

It is obvious that Mrs. Radiwker, who was 81 at that time, did not understand the issue, and was unable to remember whether, over ten years ago, she used the name Ivan before Goldfarb did. The written record did not contain the answer, although it was the most crucial element of the whole case. Mentioning 'Someone that looks familiar' or 'Ivan the Terrible from the Treblinka gas chambers' means the difference between failed or successful identification. And it was Goldfarb who could have received the clue from Mrs. Radiwker's mouth, and who was in the position to influence, directly or indirectly, all other witnesses. How can a court reach any conclusion if such crucial information is missing?

Negative results
A special problem of incomplete reporting is the suppression of negative results. In the context of the cross examination on Kudlik and Teigman, Mrs. Radiwker made a casual but revealing comment on this. She confirmed that these two witnesses did not identify Fedorenko and Demjanjuk.

Q. And then, when you were asked about a certain detail concerning that event you said: 'I don't remember now. It was a non-identification and I don't attribute any importance to it'.
A. So? It was a non-identification. It isn't relevant anymore. (JET, 2902)

Then a lengthy discussion followed on the importance of negative results, in which Judge Levine made the following statement.

If someone would show the court partial, selective information, using only what is advantageous for that investigation, to my mind that would have been unfair. Unfortunately this happens in courts in Israel almost every day. But this is another matter. At her level, as an investigator, if I understand her answer correctly, and I believe this is how the answer should be understood, she is saying: 'I as an investigator did not try to bring any influence to bear on the witnesses, to refresh their memories, to tell them what someone else had said. If he says he identifies someone, I write it down. If he says he does not identify anyone, I write it down that he didn't identify anyone'. (JET, 2905)

Thus Judge Levine's position is clearly that the investigator should report about all witnesses, whether they could identify the suspect or not, and also that the prosecution should not be allowed to bring forward only testimony about witnesses who identified the suspect if there are also witnesses who didn't. This is not what Mrs. Radiwker said, because she stated clearly that she was not interested in negative identifications. But even if we accept Judge Levine's interpretation, it must be admitted that only five eyewitnesses who produced positive identifications were questioned in the Jerusalem court: Rosenberg, Czarny, Boraks, Epstein, and Rajchman. It is simply not known how many witnesses were tested. At the Cleveland trial there were discussions about other witnesses, but they were not available for testimony. Detterman, in his memorandum for the Cleveland trial, claimed that the Trawniki picture was identified by 15 out of 33 witnesses, and the Immigration picture by 8 out of 29. Detterman comments:

From the government's response to questions posed to it by defense, it is somewhat difficult to be sure of exact figures. For example, it is not clear if those indicated as failing to make an identification also includes those persons who refused to attempt an identification or not. (Detterman, 1981)

Whatever the exact figures are, it is eminently clear that there were many witnesses, survivors of Treblinka, who did not recognize one or both pictures. Even if the investigators reported these results faithfully, which is not evident because many files are not available, then still the actual number of survivors who failed to positively identify one or both pictures was not presented by the prosecution at trials in Cleveland and Jerusalem.

SUGGESTION

Both Mrs. Radiwker and Mr. Kolar knew which picture was supposed to represent Ivan. Therefore it was possible for them to influence the responses, and the written reports reflect such undesired influences.

The time for inspection was not preset, and was in some cases extremely long. It would have been simple to continue the procedure after a 'wrong' answer, and to stop it after the identification of the target. Kolar employed this method at least once, when he interviewed Rosenberg. Rosenberg pointed to the picture of Demjanjuk, and Kolar asked him to take another look.

Another arbitrary method based on investigator knowledge is to accept or reject identifications when the phrasing used by the witness reflects a degree of uncertainty. Kolar rejected the wrong identification of Nicolai because Epstein said 'This face reminds me. . .' At the same time he accepted the identification of Demjanjuk, although Epstein had said again 'This reminds me. . .'

It was also possible to direct the attention of the witnesses to one specific picture. Mrs. Radiwker did this twice, with Turowski and Kudlik. The fact that both investigators reported these practices signifies that they were unaware of their inadmissibility. They were not dishonest, but naive. Since they saw no harm in it, they could have used the same methods more often, also without reporting it.

A remarkable misunderstanding about undue suggestion occurred throughout the Jerusalem trial. The investigators stressed many times that they asked witnesses to identify 'Ukrainians', without giving a more specific indication. Apparently they were afraid of influencing the witnesses by telling them, for instance, to look for the likeness of Ivan. In fact they were completely mistaken about this. A vague instruction to search for any person that looks familiar may lower the witnesses' response criterion, and thus increase the risk of false alarms. Witnesses should be told to look for the one person they described to the investigator. They should also be told that there is only one target, that this target is the only person they could possibly recognize, and that identification of a foil will be recorded as an error. Hence, in their anxiety not to influence the witnesses, the investigators maintained an undesirable uncertainty about the nature of the choice before them.

CONFIDENCE

How certain were the witnesses that they had really recognized Ivan? Here we are again faced with the problem of incomplete recording. Recognition of a suspect can only be accepted as legal evidence if it is immediate. Therefore we need reports about the first recognitions, not about recognitions that occurred later. Mrs. Radiwker did not report the first recognitions by Goldfarb, Turowski, and Czarny. Of the others, Rosenberg was not certain: 'I see a great resemblance; I decline to identify with certainty'. Epstein was also not certain: 'This picture reminds me strongly of Ivan'. Rajchman needed half an hour, and was only 'fairly certain'. The only immediate and certain first identifications were by Boraks, Lindwasser, and Levkowitch. At the Jerusalem trial Boraks was too old to produce a meaningful testimony; Lindwasser was dead; the testimony by Levkowitch was withdrawn. It is not unfair to conclude that out of some 30 witnesses only three were reported to be certain. These three made their identifications more than four months after the testing of Turowski, Goldfarb, and Rosenberg. They could have talked to the others at the yearly memorial meeting, but they could not be interviewed about this in court.

MULTIPLE WITNESSES

It was explained in Chapter 3 that the purpose of testing more witnesses is to allow falsification of previous positive identifications. Corroboration by further eyewitnesses does not prove the identifications correct because witnesses may make the same mistake or, worse, may have influenced each other. After the initial identifications by Turowski, Goldfarb, and Rosenberg, there were many negative results; if we believe Detterman, there were *more* negative than positive identifications. The US prosecutor did not report these negative results; nor did he voluntarily explain why they should not be accepted as proof that the initial identifications were mistaken. On the contrary, the minority of positive identifications were presented as a set of mutually reinforcing testimonies that left no doubt whatsoever. The fact that so many witnesses failed to make any identification creates a serious doubt about the identity of John Demjanjuk. In principle there are two possibilities: either those who did not identify him did not perceive or remember Ivan accurately; or those who did identify him all made the same mistake. What is the probability of these two cases? The first possibility is in fact not at all unlikely; we know from the case of Marinus De Rijke that even concentration camp survivors forget, and 40 years is a long time. But the second possibility should be a major source of concern to the court, because the investigations were conducted in such a suggestive manner that the same mistake could easily have occurred in one third of the witnesses. The photographic parades were actually showups, not lineups. The investigators could have exerted all sorts of suggestion. The identifications were separated by considerable time periods, in which the witnesses could have talked to each other. From experiences with other cases we know that these are exactly the conditions in which confirmation by successive witnesses should not be accepted as corroboration.

VIOLATION OF RULES

It is clear from the foregoing discussion that the investigators violated many of the rules proposed in Chapter 3, and that the violations were to a large extent unnecessary. Rules 3, 4, 5 and 6 were violated because the photographic lineup was in fact a mugfile inspection. Rule 7 was violated because the five witnesses who testified in court were subjected to repeated testing. Violations of Rule 11 and 12 occurred because the negative identifications were not reported. Violations of Rule 13 to 16 were due to careless dealing with the problems of multiple witnesses. The failure to obtain prior descriptions of Ivan led the investigators to violate Rules 17, 18 and 19. The careless instructions to witnesses were violations of Rules 20 and 21. The lack of training was a violation of Rule 22. The actual identity tests violated Rules 23 to 30, 32 to 33, 39 to 41, and 43 to 46. Rules 34 and 42 were violated because the official record lacks relevant information about many aspects of the test procedures and the outcomes. Finally the use of dock identification was a violation of Rule 48.

A summary of violations is listed in Table 5.1. There were 46 rules applicable to the identification of Ivan. Four of these are meant for use by the court, not the investigators. Out of the 42 remaining rules, 37 were directly or indirectly violated by the investigating authorities. Mrs. Radiwker and Mr. Kolar cannot be blamed for all these errors, because they lacked the training that is needed to conduct such complicated procedures. But that does not remove our problem: the procedures used for the identification of Ivan are notoriously invalid. Although I admit that not all of these rules are accepted as an international standard, it is easy to see that at least some of the violations are extremely worrying. I will not say that the investigative procedure was a farce, but a total farce could have violated only a few more rules.

Table 5.1: An overview of violations of the rules proposed in Chapter 3.

Number	Violation	Topic of rule
1	NA	Identification of known suspects
2	OK	No showup instead of lineup
3	V	No mugfile inspection as proof of identity
4	VI	Use no witness that looked at mugfile before
5	VI	No mugfile when proper test is possible
6	VI	No mugfile inspection before identification
7	V	No repeated identification
8	C	Identification needs corroboration
9	C	More identification is not corroborative
10	OK	Falsification should be attempted
11	V	No selective reporting
12	V	Explanation of failed identifications
13	V	Probative value of multiple witnesses
14	V	Prevent contacts among witnesses
15	V	Investigate contacts among witnesses
16	V	Exclude witnesses that had contacts
17	V	Obtain prior descriptions of the criminal
18	VI	Prior description should fit suspect

19	V	Explain which criminal is to be identified
20	V	Record instructions to witness
21	V	Debiasing instructions
22	V	Training of investigators
23	V	One suspect in a parade
24	VI	Witness knows there is only one suspect
25	VI	Separate parades for each suspect
26	VI	Witness should point to one person only
27	V	Preferably 10–12 people in lineup
28	V	All foils must fit prior description
29	VI	No use of non-fitting prior descriptions
30	VI	At least one prior description available
31	OK	No foils from homogeneous group
32	V	Mock witnesses must not guess who is suspect
33	V	Witness must not logically exclude foils
34	V	Keep material used in tests
35	NA	Photographs of live lineups
36	OK	Record identity of foils
37	NA	Video-recordings of live lineups
38	NA	Instruct participants in live lineups
39	V	Counteract transformations
40	V	Investigators must not know who is the target
41	V	Timing of presentation
42	V	Accurate recording
43	V	No feedback to witnesses
44	V	Defense counsel present
45	V	Accept only full recognitions
46	V	No recognitions after long inspection time
47	OK	No other expressions of uncertainty
48	V	No dock identification
49	C	No unjustified breach of rules
50	C	Reduced validity through breach of rules

V = violated;
VI = violation implied by other violations;
OK = not violated;
C = to be applied by the court;
NA = not applicable.

6 Ethical Aspects of Expert Testimony

Many questions were raised with respect to the ethics of expert testimony when I was required to testify in the trial of John Demjanjuk in the Jerusalem Court. These questions fitted well into the current discussions on the reliability of psychological research, the applicability of laboratory research to real life situations, the requirement of informing the courts with respect to the results of psychological research and the desirability of science serving the interests of one party in a legal battle.

The state prosecutor raised some of these questions when he examined me in Jerusalem. Any failure to respond to these questions would seriously reduce the value of an expert witness's testimony, therefore discussing these sensitive matters could not be avoided. All expert witnesses should have considered these initial questions prior to testifying and should therefore base their testimonies on their own philosophical standpoints. These are by definition of a highly personal nature, but experts should not be shown to be testifying and acting in conflict with their own theoretical positions. For example an expert who considers that laboratory research cannot be applied in a real life setting should not claim that in a specific criminal case cross-racial recognition problems impeded a reliable identification. Nor should an expert who feels that a scientist should never be biased to one side be willing to testify and present a biased selection of the relevant literature.

Before opening a discussion of these questions I will describe the model of Bayesian decision making as a context that will help to clarify the problems and the positions adopted by different authors. Only thereafter will I discuss the three questions that constitute the substance of this chapter:

1. Is psychological research reliable and sufficiently valid to be applied in the courtroom?
2. Do courts need to be told about matters they might know very well anyway?
3. Is it acceptable for a scientist to be called as an expert witness for the defense of someone who is accused of killing 850,000 people?

There are also some issues that defy scientific treatment. One of these is the statement that it is useless to testify in a case like Demjanjuk's because the Israeli judges would convict him anyway, irrespective of what might be brought up in court. This is of course a terrible accusation against the legal system of Israel, and against the judges involved in this case. I will not discuss such accusations because I feel that first of all they are totally unfounded; secondly, if they were true, one should not give in to injustice by remaining silent. If experts have something important to say, they have a moral obligation to do so.

Another argument put to me by many people is that if Demjanjuk is not Ivan, he is still a Ukrainian, who probably served the Germans in another way. Therefore it would not be a terrible mistake to convict him, and any effort to defend him would be a waste. This argument has nothing to do with scientific viewpoints. It simply reflects a prejudice that runs counter to my most basic beliefs about justice, fair trial, and human rights. One cannot convict a person because, if he did not commit the crime he was charged with, he probably did something else. Neither can one convict a person for belonging to an ethnic group. However, those among us who are prepared to act as expert witnesses in cases in which their expertise might assist the defense of the accused should prepare themselves for confrontations with such opinions, voiced openly and in letters, or left as unspoken thoughts and emotions.

THE BAYESIAN MODEL OF A CRIMINAL TRIAL

The Bayesian model of legal fact-finding has been discussed before by many authors (e.g. Weinstein, Mansfield, Abram & Berger, 1983; Wagenaar, 1988b). I will present it here as a context that helps to understand the different kinds of information that play a part in a criminal trial, and the tasks of the various actors in this process. It is not my intention to present the Bayesian model as an accurate description of how judges think, and even less as a prescriptive rule, telling how judges *should* think.

In the case of Demjanjuk there are two mutually exclusive hypotheses: Demjanjuk is Ivan, or he is not Ivan. I will designate these hypotheses by H_i and H_{ni}, and the corresponding probabilities for these hypotheses of being true by $p(H_i)$ and $p(H_{ni})$. Neither of these two probabilities can equal zero because that would automatically put the other at one. It is not certain that Demjanjuk is Ivan, nor is it certain that he is not Ivan. In an Israeli court the judges do not know anything about the case before the trial starts. They can only use information that is presented to them publicly, in court. As a matter of principle it is assumed that the accused is innocent, until guilt is proved. But it is not assumed that innocence is certain, because then no amount of proof could change that position. Hence it can be said that the *prior odds* $p(H_i)/p(H_{ni})$, which are the odds before receiving the evidence, are very, very low to begin with. But they are above zero, since both $p(H_i)$ and $p(H_{ni})$ are above zero.

The evidence about the identity of Demjanjuk consists of eyewitness testimony, designated by E. The question is, what are the *posterior odds* after the reception of the evidence E? The posterior probabilities are designated by $p(H_i|E)$ and $p(H_{ni}|E)$. This is pronounced as the probability that H_i (or H_{ni}) is true, given the reception of E. The posterior odds are expressed by $p(H_i|E)/p(H_{ni}|E)$.

The process of judicial decision making can be characterized as the transformation of prior odds into posterior odds. How is this transformation achieved? Bayes' rule prescribes the following computational procedure (see Vlek and Wagenaar, 1979)

$$\frac{p(H_i|E)}{p(H_{ni}|E)} = \frac{p(H_i)}{p(H_{ni})} * \frac{p(E|H_i)}{p(E|H_{ni})} \qquad (6.1)$$

Or in words: the posterior odds are equal to the prior odds, multiplied by the likelihood ratio. The likelihood ratio consists of the likelihoods that the evidence E would be obtained if H_i (or H_{ni}) were true. The likelihood ratio represents the diagnostic value of the evidence, in our case the diagnostic value of the outcome of identification tests. In Chapter 3 we have already mentioned that the diagnosticity of lineup procedures equals the likelihood ratio. In the case of Demjanjuk we have estimated that the effective lineup size was not above 1.0, and this puts the likelihood ratio close to 1.5. With such a likelihood ratio the impact of an identification test is that the prior odds are only increased by 50 percent.

The Bayesian model allows for a clear distinction between the task of the court and the task of expert witnesses. Prior odds and posterior odds are the domain of the court. Prior odds represent its neutrality or prejudice, its preconceived convictions about the probability that certain kinds of people commit certain kinds of crimes, or that the police can be trusted to accuse people only when they are guilty. Posterior odds constitute the judgment, the evaluation based on facts presented at the trial, an opinion which is in principle personal. Posterior odds are never infinitely large because there is always a slight possibility that the court is mistaken. A court should not request complete certainty before reaching a conclusion, but only posterior odds that are sufficiently high.

Likelihoods are the domain of the experts. How likely is it that a witness will identify a suspect when the suspect is, in fact, not the real criminal? Likelihoods can be obtained from statistical surveys, or from experimental studies, and should take into account the specific aspects of the case. In the case of Ivan these likelihoods should take into account factors that may have impeded or assisted perception and memory of the witnesses, and factors related to the testing of these processes. The two extreme conclusions that could be reached in such testimony are:

- It is very unlikely that witnesses would say they recognize Demjanjuk if he is not the same person as Ivan.
- It is very likely that witnesses would say they recognize Demjanjuk even if in fact he is not the same person as Ivan.

In reality an expert's statement might not be one of those extremes. But irrespective of the shade that is chosen, the testimony should share one property with these extremes, which is that it is in the form of $E|H$: the likelihood of obtaining evidence when a hypothesis is true. Statements in the complementary form $H|E$, the likelihood that a hypothesis is true given the evidence, are in the domain of the court. This excludes a large number of questions that are not suitable topics for expert testimony. Did the procedures used by the Israeli investigators promote the erroneous identification of Demjanjuk? Do the horrors of Treblinka ensure accurate memory? Do witnesses remember the face of Ivan after 35 years? Are the witnesses mistaken when they say they recognize Demjanjuk? Is Demjanjuk lying when he denies being Ivan? Is Demjanjuk Ivan the Terrible? Answers to these questions would all be in the form $H|E$, and would therefore be outside the domain of admissible expert testimony. The court should prevent the prosecutor and the defense attorney from asking such questions; if they are asked, the answers should not be accepted in evidence.

The distinction between the form $H|E$ and $E|H$ can be quite subtle, as is demonstrated by the following example.

- ($H|E$) Given the conditions in which the identifications were made, there is no sufficient proof that Demjanjuk is Ivan.
- ($E|H$) The conditions under which Demjanjuk was identified as Ivan are known to have produced mistaken identifications before.

In the first statement something is said about the probability that Demjanjuk is Ivan, given the identifications. In the second it is said that such identifications are likely, given innocence. Here are more examples of this subtle distinction. I present these because the distinction has direct consequences for the role of expert witnesses in the judicial process, and for the ethics of expert testimony. Experts who cross the thin line between $E|H$ and $H|E$ may suddenly find themselves in an undesired role, violating basic rules of ethics, and eliciting justified criticism both from colleagues and the general public.

- ($H|E$) According to the literature on eyewitness reliability the identifications do not prove that Demjanjuk was in Treblinka.
- ($E|H$) According to the literature on eyewitness reliability it is likely that the witnesses would identify Demjanjuk, when in fact he was never in Treblinka.

- ($H|E$) An analysis of mistakes in previous Nazi crime trials makes it very likely that the Treblinka survivors will remember the faces of their former guards accurately.
- ($E|H$) An analysis of mistakes in previous Nazi crime trials reveals that survivors of death camps tend not to identify innocent outsiders as their former guards.

- ($H|E$) The suggestive photographic lineup caused the witnesses to make mistakes.
- ($E|H$) Such suggestive photographic lineups are known to confuse witnesses.

It should be stressed that these statements illustrate only the incorrect and correct *forms*; even if the form is correct the content might still be wrong.

The last example is a clear demonstration of the division of tasks between court and experts. The expert can determine whether a photographic lineup was suggestive, and what in the past the effects of suggestive lineups have been. These statements can be refined to reflect the exact conditions of the present case. It is even possible to conduct experiments that mimic the conditions of the present case almost exactly, with the specific purpose of arriving at valid conclusions. But in no way can the expert determine whether the witnesses were, in fact, influenced by the suggestive properties of the lineup. It is still possible that the witnesses recognized the suspect straightaway, and that they would also have recognized the suspect if there had been no suggestion. The court can be told about the reliability of identifications in general, but it must decide itself whether it will accept this specific identification as reliable or not.

THE RELIABILITY AND VALIDITY OF PSYCHOLOGICAL RESEARCH

It has been argued that the results of psychological research are generally unreliable. Research outcomes are not robust, which means that different authors report different results, or even opposite results. This lack of robustness is an obstacle to application in forensic practice. A clear example of such an encompassing critique is provided by Donald Bersoff in the Maryland Law Review (1979). He concluded:

The probative value and admissibility of each level of psychological testimony is suspect. Although psychological expert witnesses may be properly qualified in terms of their education and experience, these criteria do not assure that the scientific underpinnings of such testimony are valid. Psychological judgments are not as accurate as the courts presume them to be, and diagnoses based upon a psychologist's observations are, at the very least, questionable. For reasons that remain obscure, the courts have failed to apply to psychology the standard used to evaluate the admissibility of novel types of scientific evidence. Because the courts have tacitly taken judicial notice of psychology as a *bona fide* scientific discipline, there is no opportunity at trial to assail the underlying accuracy of such judgments in terms of their reliability and validity (p. 598).

It should be noted that this conclusion refers to clinical judgments about insanity of the accused, the mental status of a victim, the risk that a convicted person can become violent again, and the like. Such judgments are based on intuition, or on psychological tests with limited reliability and validity. In fact Bersoff argued that psychological judgments of experienced clinicians may not be superior to those of novices, or even lay persons. There is an abundance of studies that serve to demonstrate the limitations of predictions made by psychologists. But these limitations are not really the issue. The more worrying aspect is that psychologists are apparently allowed to state that a person was insane when he committed the crime, or that a person has mentally suffered from being the victim of a crime, or that a convict will not become violent again. Such statements are obviously in the form H|E, and are therefore inadmissible, irrespective of whether they are valid and reliable or not. Invalid or unreliable conclusions are a threat to justice when they are pronounced in the form H|E because they may replace the court's judgment. Nobody wants invalid or unreliable judgments. The harm done by invalid or unreliable statements in the form E|H can be much smaller because they will never substitute the court's judgment. Later I will discuss how a court can take into account the limited validity and reliability of statements expressed in the proper form.

An illustration of the confusion between H|E and E|H is offered by McCloskey and Egeth's attack on the role of experimental psychologists as experts on questions of eyewitness reliability (McCloskey and Egeth, 1983) These authors conclude that expert testimony may have little benefit for the justice system. Their line of argument is summarized in a mock cross examination in which an experimental psychologist seems to be in a very awkward position. The reader enters the interrogation shortly after the psychologist has explained that identification of a criminal by eyewitnesses can be mistaken. The expert raises the issues of general accuracy of eyewitnesses, effects of weapon focus and stress, and of problems related to cross-racial identification. The prosecutor, instructed by another expert, attempts to undermine the testimony by eliciting the following statements from the expert:

- Some studies show that subjects can make accurate identifications.
- Laboratory experiments are deliberately arranged to make accuracy low.
- It is not possible to predict which witnesses will be accurate and which will not.
- There are not many studies on the effect of weapon focus.
- The difficulty of cross-racial identification makes a difference in accuracy of only 10 percent.
- The effects of stress on identification are not always consistent.

Now why all these attenuations of the original testimony are so important becomes clear when the last question is fired at the expert who is, by now, very timid:

Prosecutor: How can these vague principles be of any help to the jury, Dr. Smith, when you, with all your knowledge and experience, cannot use them to tell whether a witness was accurate or not?

The last question is misleading and wrong. It is not the expert's task to evaluate whether a witness was accurate. The jury or the court should make this judgment because the problem is in the form H|E: is it true that the witness saw the suspect at the scene of the crime, given that he identified the suspect in a lineup? The expert can only assist the court or the jury by explaining which conditions favor the correct identification of guilty suspects, and which favor the mistaken identification of innocent suspects. The correct question would have been:

Prosecutor: How can these vague principles be of any help to the jury, when they evaluate whether a witness was accurate or not?

Let us see how Dr. Smith could have responded to the list of accusations of McCloskey and Egeth.

Sometimes witnesses are accurate
The argument seems to be that statements about witness accuracy are probabilistic, not deterministic. There is

nothing wrong with that in the context of the Bayesian model. The posterior odds on which the verdict is based is also of a probabilistic nature. It is very useful to know that suggestive lineups have in the past increased the likelihood of mistaken identifications. Such information is related to $p(E|H_{ni})$ which influences the diagnostic value of the identification test. This diagnostic value is never zero or infinite, and something better than a probabilistic statement about it cannot be expected. Psychologists can not be blamed for the fact that the diagnostic value of identification tests is a probabilistic quantity. They did not propose or instigate this method of investigation. McCloskey and Egeth confuse the message with the messenger. The police chose a method with a limited diagnostic value; when psychologists explain this problem, are they the ones that must be dropped instead of the method? Problems arise only when the expert misrepresents the likelihoods, or replaces them by certainties. But in that case the expert would be dishonest, or not qualified.

Laboratory experiments are invalid
There is some truth in the statement that laboratory studies on accuracy of perception and memory must avoid ceiling and floor effects, i.e. scores that are close to 100 or 0 percent, because the effects of experimental manipulations cannot be measured in these extreme regions. But the argument should not be reversed: accuracy scores between 25 and 75 percent do not always result from deliberately chosen unrealistic conditions. The large majority of eyewitness studies reviewed by Shapiro and Penrod (1986, see Chapter 2) were planned to represent real life conditions, not to yield intermediate scores. The resulting average scores of about 70 percent correct identifications in target-present lineups is representative of these realistic conditions.

A more fundamental problem is raised by King (1986) in his book on the undesirability of psychologists in the courtroom. His principal argument is that experimental studies are doomed to fail because the underlying questions cannot reflect the questions that are raised in the realistic social context of the courtroom. Without entering a long and detailed discussion about this claim, I will say that the statement obviously cannot be true for all types of expert testimony. When a doctor testifies that, according to a laboratory test, the blood group of the victim was A+, no one would object that laboratory tests are generally invalid. Hence the validity of laboratory research depends on the question that is asked. Questions about the memories of death camp survivors are not easily resolved in the laboratory, and maybe not at all. The same may be true for the recall of details of an armed robbery, although it might be possible to simulate armed robberies even in the laboratory. But our problem is not related to such estimator variables. We are concerned about the methods used by police investigators when they are testing the memories of witnesses in a laboratory situation. If we find that certain methods decrease the reliability of recall in a range of laboratory situations, why should a court then make the risky assumption that such effects are totally absent when police investigators run their tests in their laboratories? Even if a certain proportion of the validity is lost by going from the psychological laboratory to the police laboratory, then there is still information in the proportion that is preserved.

Which witness is accurate?
There is considerable truth in the argument that the expert does not know which witness will tell the truth. But it is not the expert's task to make such assessments. The expert can only present information about variables that are possibly relevant. The actual assessment of witness reliability is in the domain of the court.

Insufficient empirical evidence
It is true that in some areas there is not a sufficiently large body of empirical evidence. But this is a problem that can be discussed by the expert. In fact experts should be forced to reveal the scientific material on which their testimony is based, and in that process it would immediately become clear whether the empirical evidence is substantial or not. A good example is the lack of literature on the memories of concentration camp survivors, which caused me to exclude from my testimony any statement on this matter.

Again, problems can arise only if an expert were prepared to misrepresent the scientific facts. But that would reflect badly upon this expert, not upon psychology as an area for expert testimony.

Some effects are small

I fail to see why that would create any problem. Small influences can be represented as being small. Let us assume that indeed the problem of cross-racial identification is limited to a 10 percent difference. The small effect means that the diagnostic value of an identification test is not much affected by the presence of cross-racial differences. Why would it be wrong to tell a court about this? In my opinion this is exactly what the court or the jury needs to know: the problem of cross-racial differences hardly affects the diagnostic value of the test. Even if cross-racial differences have no effect at all, it would be necessary to inform the court about this. A testimony about $E|H$ can only go wrong when the expert reports the wrong values. But that would again be unprofessional, or merely dishonest.

Some effects are inconsistent

There is not much against inconsistent effects, provided that they are reported as such. If a factor such as stress during the crime has inconsistent effects, the conclusion must be that this factor should not affect the diagnostic value of the identification, unless it can be determined how large the effect has been in the actual situation. The statement that the horror of concentration camp experiences did in comparable cases not have the effect of consistently increasing the reliability of identifications might prevent judges from unrealistically increasing the diagnostic value of identifications by surviving witnesses. Reporting that some variables have inconsistent or small effects is as meaningful as the reporting of consistent or large effects because the information is still relevant for the definition of the diagnostic value of the evidence.

AVAILABILITY OF RELEVANT KNOWLEDGE

The real issue, when validity and reliability are at stake, is whether an expert is sufficiently knowledgeable and honest enough to represent the existing know-how in a fair manner. There is no *a priori* reason why psychologists should in this respect be trusted less than medical doctors, engineers or lawyers. But a relevant difference between these disciplines might be that engineering, medicine, and law are more sophisticated sciences than psychology. Maybe a psychologist should not be allowed to testify in the case of John Demjanjuk because psychology as a science has nothing to offer. With respect to estimator variables related to the specific situation of death camp survivors this argument could be true: psychological theory does not allow reliable predictions about their situation, and there is not a substantial body of empirical evidence. It is not clear why information is lacking: possibly the topic is simply not suitable for experimental study, or maybe we never realized that we might be asked such questions. The truth is that in fact psychologists cannot testify about the impact of estimator variables upon the diagnostic value of the identification tests in this specific case. But for system variables the picture is different. There is a vast literature on system variables, many of the reported outcomes are demonstrably robust, and we possess reliable estimations of the effect sizes. It is noteworthy that McCloskey and Egeth's objections are directed exclusively to testimony about estimator variables. Does this mean that they tacitly approve of testimony about system variables?

A discussion of system variables leads automatically to an analysis of the *methods* used in the identification texts. Examples of this are the construction of the test material, the instructions to witnesses, the avoidance of suggestive influencing, the delays in reporting. Psychologists have learned much about such matters in the last 50 years. Although we do not always agree about theories, or about the robustness of experimental outcomes, it is much easier to reach agreement about certain types of methodological errors. Few psychologists will disagree with me when I state that a lineup should not contain implausible foils; that witnesses should be warned about the possible absence of the target; that investigators should not point at one participant specifically; and that reports should not be written seven years after the test. Hence it is my sincere conviction that system variables which affect the reliability of identifications constitute a proper area for expert testimony by experimental psychologists.

IS EXPERT TESTIMONY NEEDED?

The second question to be discussed in this chapter is whether psychologists possess reliable and valid information that is unknown to judges and juries. Are these intelligent lay people unaware of such simple rules as that lineups should be fair, that witnesses should be properly instructed, that investigators should not make suggestions, and that reports should be reliable? McCloskey and Egeth argue that judges and juries do already possess such information, and that expert testimony on such matters is not needed. They state that:

There is virtually no empirical evidence that people are unaware of the problems with eyewitness testimony. Further there appears to be no reason to assume *a priori* that people are not cognizant of these problems. Cases of mistaken identification are often widely publicized and wrongful conviction on the basis of mistaken or perjured eyewitness testimony is a rather common theme in fiction. In addition, there is no consensus within the legal community that jurors are unaware of the unreliability of eyewitnesses and consequently give too much credence to eyewitness testimony. For example, in ruling against the admission of expert psychological testimony, the trial judge in the case of *People v. Guzman* stated: 'It is something that everyone knows about, the problems of identification. The jurors here were well questioned regarding their experience . . . with having mistakenly identified people. Everyone knows these things happen.' Thus in the absence of evidence that jurors are unaware of the unreliability of eyewitnesses testimony, the conclusion that jurors are too willing to believe eyewitnesses cannot legitimately be drawn from research demonstrating that eyewitnesses are often inaccurate. (p. 551)

One argument supporting the idea that judges and jurors need help is that wrongful convictions still occur. McCloskey and Egeth say about this that convictions are by definition not 100 percent safe. Wrongful convictions should be avoided as much as possible, but will not disappear. They occur although the court or the jury may be very much aware of the problems of eyewitness identification. Hence the occurrence of wrongful convictions cannot be used as an argument supporting the admission of expert testimony.

I think that McCloskey and Egeth would admit that the quoted reasoning is based on some sort of common sense, whereas the knowledge and attitudes of jury members and judges could in fact be studied empirically. One of the first experiments that explored this problem was conducted by Elizabeth Loftus (1974). Mock juries received a description of a robbery-murder case. A first group was given only physical evidence of guilt. Not more than 18 percent of the jurors decided to convict the accused. A second group received the same physical evidence, plus the information that the accused was identified by an eyewitness. In this condition 72 percent of the jurors were willing to convict. To the third group again the physical evidence and the eyewitness identification was presented. Additionally it was explained that the witness had not been wearing his glasses the day of the robbery; since he had vision poorer than 20/400, he could not possibly have seen the face of the robber from where he stood. In this condition 68 percent of the jurors were willing to convict. Loftus argued that the discrediting of eyewitness testimony did not apparently have the desired effect. Jurors remained convinced of the defendant's guilt, although there was only the physical evidence, which convinced not more than 18 percent of the jurors in the physical evidence only condition.

McCloskey and Egeth report a number of studies that undermine this argument in different ways. First there are studies demonstrating that jurors do not always give too much weight to eyewitness testimony. However, a recent study by Cutler, Penrod and Stuve (1988) involving 321 subjects showed convincingly that people are generally insensitive to facts that decrease the reliability of eyewitness identification. They do not think that the reliability of identifications is influenced when the criminal was disguised by a hat, when the criminal carried a gun, when the witness was experiencing a high level of stress, or when the retention interval was long. Neither did subjects doubt the credibility of identifications more when witnesses were exposed to mugshots before the identification test, when lineup instructions were biased, when the number of foils was small, and when the foils were not plausible. Thus subjects appeared to have little understanding of both estimator and system variables. The only aspect of testimony that influenced mock jurors' acceptance was witness confidence. The reader should by now be aware of the fact that witness confidence is only weakly related to accuracy. Hence I believe strongly that Loftus' argument is still not disproved. And, if not disproved, it would be wise for a court to assume that the danger could be real: it is not certain that people are aware of factors that render identification by eyewitnesses reliable or unreliable.

The second argument launched by McCloskey and Egeth is that the testimony of an expert does not increase a jury's ability to discriminate between accurate and mistaken witnesses. The purpose of expert testimony is not to discredit eyewitnesses in general, but to help a jury to assess the reliability of specific eyewitnesses. If experts cannot do that, their testimony can be dismissed as a futile enterprise. This argument has two sides to it. One is that experts do not know which factors render identifications reliable or unreliable. This allegation is untrue: there is sufficient and robust empirical material related to eyewitness reliability that can help to assess likelihood ratios. Improvement of likelihood ratios means better discrimination between accurate and mistaken witnesses.

The second side to the argument is that experts are bad communicators; although they have the relevant knowledge, they are unable to transfer that information to juries. The original experiment of Loftus (1974) could be interpreted that way: the third group gave too much credence to eyewitness identification not because they lacked the relevant insight to begin with, but because the expert failed to give them this insight. Even if that is true, I find the argument surprising. Do McClosky and Egeth mean that defendants have no right to assistance from experts simply because laboratory studies showed that juries are unable to utilize the information? Would the logical conclusion not be that experts, if they have something important to say, should find better ways of saying it?

The best argument that courts and juries need to be told by experts about problems of eyewitness identification is that police investigators frequently violate the rules for identification procedures. It is difficult to tell from my own experience how often such violations occur because the sample of cases that are brought to my attention may constitute the exception rather than the rule. But then, even if mistaken identity is an exceptional problem, the rules are meant to protect suspects against misjudgments in such exceptional situations. The cases in which experimental psychologists testify may be exceptional, but that does not mean that in these exceptional cases such testimony is useless. I agree with McCloskey and Egeth if they intended to say that psychologists should not testify in all cases of disputed identity. But the sample of cases that have occurred in my own experience lends sufficient support to the statement that the expertise of psychologists is needed in at least some cases.

The case of John Demjanjuk is a suitable demonstration of this tenet. Many guidelines outlined in Chapter 3 were not followed, and the investigators saw no harm in it. In fact the deviation from the preferred guidelines seems to be standard practice. And the extent of this deviation gives us greater cause for concern when we consider the fact that these investigators are not lay persons. Their errors reflect what professionals do not know about eyewitness identification. Why should it be assumed that juries and judges would be better informed than these professionals?

The Cleveland court deciding about Demjanjuk's citizenship was confronted with a 'Government's motion *in limine* to bar the testimony of defendant's expert psychologist and character witnesses'. I will concentrate on the testimony of the psychologist, Douglas Detterman, the expert on identification who prepared the memorandum discussed in the previous chapter. The motion to bar the testimony was prepared by Allan A. Ryan, the director of OSI, which had

ordered the investigation, and which was responsible for
the mistake in the case of Frank Walus. The investigative
methods in the cases of Walus, Fedorenko, and Demjanjuk
were very similar. Witnesses were proved to be wrong in
the cases of Walus and Fedorenko. Would Judge Battisti,
presiding over the Cleveland court, see fit to consult an
expert on this matter in the case of John Demjanjuk?

The reason why Ryan moved to bar Detterman's testimony was that the court could not receive 'appreciable help'
from such testimony, which is required by the Federal Rules
of Evidence. In order to prove this it was argued that the
court did not need help because Detterman's message would
be within the common knowledge of the average laymen.
Moreover it would be impossible for Detterman to comment
on the reliability of a particular witness. Such reliability
should be tested by cross examination.

In the instant case, it can be expected that the defendant will attack
the eyewitness testimony against him by impugning the accuracy of the
witnesses' recall after 40 years and by exploring the effect of their experience at Treblinka upon their perceptions. As in any other case, these
matters may be fully probed on cross examination. Based on the testimony of the witnesses, on direct and cross examination, the Court is fully
capable of reaching a decision as to their credibility. The assistance of
an expert witness in judging their recall is neither required nor proper.
(p. 4 of Government's motion)

There are four reasons why this motion could elicit an incorrect interpretation. First it is not true that Detterman
intended to question the reliability of a witness's memory
after 40 years. His memorandum did not discuss such estimator variables at all, but was strictly limited to system
variables. These are the variables that relate to the methods
of testing, and there is no reason why a court should be
shielded from a careful scrutiny of investigative methods. It
is illuminating that the Government's motion stipulates only
that 'it can be expected' that the expert would discuss estimator variables.

Second, it is not true that expertise on system variables
is within the common knowledge of the average lay person.
The best proof is the large number of procedural weaknesses

in the Demjanjuk investigation. Without much extra effort, but with a little more attention to appropriate scientific standards, the investigators could have built a much stronger case, if Demjanjuk was really Ivan. They failed to do so because this sort of procedural expertise was not even common knowledge to these professionals.

Third, it is not true that all relevant information concerning identification methods can be obtained through cross examination of eyewitnesses. They may appear perfectly reliable in court, while the methods used to obtain their testimony may have been highly suggestive.

But the most misleading element is the suggestion that Detterman might want to assess the witnesses' reliability, which would be an assessment in the form $H|E$. The motion suggested that the expert, if permitted to testify, would invade the province of the court. But a good expert would not do that, and a good presiding judge would not allow it. The danger of an expert making statements in the form $H|E$ is always present, but that is no reason to bar all experts. It is the judge's task to explain to prosecutor, defense counsel, and expert what sort of questions may be asked, and what sort of answers may be given. Detterman's memorandum is definitely in the proper form. It presents an assessment of the likelihood that witnesses would identify Demjanjuk when he is not the same person as Ivan. That is, of $E|H_{ni}$.

However, Judge Battisti did not agree with this opinion; he barred Detterman from testifying, and as a result there was no expert who commented on the procedures described in Chapter 4.

Investigators responsible for the conduct of identification procedures can easily make mistakes, and such mistakes could seriously influence the outcome of the tests. Detailed knowledge with respect to the testing of human perception and memory is in the domain of experimental psychologists, and not in the domain of police investigators, public prosecutors, defense attorneys, eyewitnesses, jurors, and judges. It would be perfectly proper for a psychologist to testify on such a matter, provided that the testimony is in the correct form.

TESTIFYING FOR THE DEFENSE

The role of an expert witness
Is it proper that scientists let themselves be drawn into the interests of one party in a legal battle? An extensive discussion of this question is presented in Elizabeth Loftus' paper: 'Experimental psychologist as advocate or impartial educator' (1986). The question she asks is whether experts in court should act as impartial educators, presenting objective information that may support or harm both parties, or as advocates of one side, who are willing to proffer only what is in the interest of the party that requested their assistance. Loftus presented a large number of arguments for and against both positions and left the question undecided. She suggested that evolutionary mechanisms will finally vindicate those experts who adopted the correct role.

In the framework of the Bayesian model of a trial process it is perfectly clear that experts can never be advocates. It is their task to tell the court about $E|H$, that is about facts resulting from scientific research. They should never be permitted to present selectively only a part of these results, or to misrepresent them. Even expert witnesses pledge to tell the whole truth. Of course it can happen that two scientists disagree about what the facts mean. There might even be a 'battle of experts' in court. But such a battle would be based upon a common understanding of the relevant scientific literature.

An expert can only give testimony when it is clear that there is a scientific question to which the answer can be formulated in the form $E|H$. There should also be a substantial empirical basis that allows reliable answers. Scientists should not be willing to testify if these conditions are not fulfilled. The question 'Are the identifications correct?' is inappropriate. It is a judicial question, not a scientific question, and its answer can only be given in the wrong form. 'How reliable are identifications after 40 years?' is a scientific question that could be answered by assessment of $p(E|H_i)$ and $p(E|H_{ni})$; unfortunately there is not a sufficient empirical basis to enable such assessments. The question 'Was the photographic lineup fair?' is fully within the scientific domain of an experimental psychologist, and leads to an answer in the form $E|H$, and can be answered on the basis of sufficient empirical knowledge. The answer would not depend on which side hired the expert, and does not compromise the neutral position of science in any way.

In most cases experts are not invited to testify as friends of the court. They are acting on behalf of the prosecution or the defense, and this could threaten their neutral position because all parties involved, including the experts themselves, might misconceive what is expected of an expert in court. An expert invited and paid by the defense could be perceived as someone who intends to defend the accused. But this would be wrong. The expert intends to answer a scientific question. It is immaterial whether the answer helps or damages the accused. The reason why the defense invited the expert is the expectation that the neutral answer to a scientific question will support the defense case, not that the expert will support the defense by giving a biased answer to the question. In fact it is desirable to discredit expert witnesses if they are shown to be biased.

In most cases the relevant scientific knowledge is rather complex and should be presented in its full complexity. The result could be that the inviting party is not unequivocally pleased with everything the expert has said. But that cannot be helped, and the experts should definitely not permit the inviting party to conceal certain elements of the testimony. One way to prevent this is to submit a written deposition in which all relevant points are mentioned. The case of John Demjanjuk is a good example of this problem. Although my testimony was requested by the defense, I wished to tell the court that the 40 years retention period was not a principal obstacle to obtaining reliable testimony. On the contrary, I described in my written deposition the research by Bahrick et al. (1975), which demonstrated that recognition of classmates is still above 80 percent correct after 50 years.

The likelihood ratio $p(E|H_i)/p(E|H_{ni})$ which describes the diagnostic value of identification by eyewitnesses is not defined by expert testimony only. The rules of evidence enshrined in the law have something to say about it. For instance, the suggestion put forward by the Devlin Committee that the burden of proof should be increased in cases of disputed identity is in fact a suggestion that a low *a priori* diagnostic value should be assigned to identification tests. Judges and juries will also have their own preset values, for instance, as argued by McCloskey and Egeth, because much publicity is given to cases of wrongful conviction. In the extreme an expert may hope to replace these intuitive values by some better founded ones. A more modest objective would be to influence the preset values in a direction indicated by scientific knowledge. When scientific knowledge is lacking, inconclusive, or outright conflicting, the expert should explain that situation to the court. There is nothing wrong if an expert points out to the court that science has no definite answer to an otherwise legitimate question, and the effect of such testimony should be that the preset diagnostic values remain unchanged.

Public perception

Although the implication of the Bayesian framework is clearly that experts, as long as they limit themselves to honest, unbiased, and complete statements in the form E|H, cannot be accused of acting for the defense, there is still the problem that the general public might perceive the involvement of an expert in a different perspective. The best example is provided in the short article 'Trials of an expert witness', published by Elizabeth Loftus in *Newsweek* (1987). She was asked to appear as a defense witness in the case of Ivan and decided to refuse. Here are her reasons.

One of the first reactions to the idea that I might testify at the Ivan trial in Israel came from Jeremy, the 11-year-old son of my closest friend. Jeremy instructed his mother to 'tell Beth that if she helps Ivan, we won't be her friend any more'. Jeremy's mother, a sensible and usually serene psychologist, made her own views clear at lunch one day when she screamed at me: 'How could you? Don't you believe in anything? . . He's probably guilty!'

Jeremy and his mother could well be fictional characters, but I have been on the receiving end of exactly the same reactions, and the problem is clear: people see the expert witness as someone who is helping one party instead of the court. Moreover people allow themselves an opinion about guilt or innocence of the suspect, and this opinion determines their attitude with respect to expert testimony. An innocent suspect is entitled to assistance by experts, a guilty suspect is not. It does not matter that guilt or innocence cannot be established prior to the trial, and maybe not without the assistance of the experts. It also does not bother people who pronounce a judgment prior to the trial that they are unfamiliar with the specifics of the case.

I had ample opportunity to interview those who opposed my involvement as an expert witness because they came forward voluntarily. One of the questions I asked them was which proportion of the witnesses had recognized Demjanjuk. Without exception they responded that they thought the five witnesses who testified in Jerusalem were the only witnesses. None of them had troubled to consider the case any closer, but still they saw fit to pronounce a judgment. It is not my intention to ridicule the feelings of the general public. Such feelings are very real, and impossible to prevent. And in an extreme case it is very understandable that an expert should decide that such feelings should not be hurt, even when they are based on ignorance.

The objection that the suspect is probably guilty presents a more difficult logical problem. This position signifies not only the belief that lay people can decide about guilt or innocence without the complete information that will be presented in court, but also that a court will not reach a better decision by using more information. The statement 'He's probably guilty' means that $p(H_i)/p(H_{ni})$ is extremely high. The fear is that expert testimony might affect the court's posterior odds, so that $p(H_i|E)/p(H_{ni}|E)$ will come out lower, and it is assumed that such a revision of opinion would be wrong. It is claimed that a court should accept prior odds as definitive instead of going through a process of revision of opinion.

Another interpretation of the objection is that there is a possibility that the court would acquit Demjanjuk while he is guilty, and that the expert witness would increase this probability. This is true in principle, although it would very much depend on the contents of the testimony. But at the same time such testimony would decrease the probability that an innocent suspect is convicted. The objection reveals that the cost of allowing the real Ivan to go free by far outweighs the cost of convicting an innocent man. There is no argument against this sort of reasoning because the assessments are highly personal. But one individual's personal assessments, or even a whole nation's assessments, cannot remove a suspect's right to his defense.

The objection is also confusing the message and the messenger. Suppose that a guilty suspect is identified only on the basis of mugshot inspection by a single witness; that subsequently an expert convinces the court that this procedure is not reliable; that the court decides then that identity is not established; and that, therefore, the accused should be acquitted. The result is that a guilty person is acquitted, and the public could consider that as a failure of justice. But the expert did the job required by the principles of fair trial. The message that there is insufficient evidence may not be welcome, but the messenger should not be blamed for it.

I fear that the emotional disapproval of a person's willingness to act as a defense witness in Nazi crime cases is elicited by the suggestion that experts are advocates instead of impartial educators. It might even be the case that experts have behaved as advocates before, by giving biased answers to the questions posed to them. If that is true, the public cannot be blamed for disliking experts who are willing to appear as defense witnesses in Ivan's case, and experts cannot be blamed for taking this dislike into consideration. Loftus said about this in her *Newsweek* article:

In the world of principle, we believe in the presumption of innocence. We believe, as the great jurist Sir William Blackstone once said, that it is better to let 10 guilty people go free than to convict one innocent person. Yet when we enter the world of Ivan, we realize that it matters very much what these 10 guilty people are guilty of. . . I decided to leave this case to my colleagues. The cost of testifying as a defense witness would have been too great for the people I love most.

My own solution to this problem was different, and I realize that this was a matter of personal choice, for which there are no normative prescriptions. After a careful study of the immense file, I chose to act as an expert witness summoned by the defense of John Demjanjuk because I felt that some matters had to be presented in court. No individual scientist could be forced to testify in this case. But what about the obligations of science as a collective? What if all psychologists, for personal reasons, refused to say the things that had to be said? Loftus quoted Emerson, who said that 'A foolish consistency is the hobgoblin of little minds.' What if all provisional expert witnesses would adopt this canon as an excuse for not testifying? Would not the basic right of the accused to their defense be endangered? And how do we know whether decisions that are consistent with this right are foolish? Can the canon be reversed, by saying that consistency with a moral principle proves one's littleness? Emerson's quote helped Loftus, it did not help me. I felt that there were good reasons for testifying, and that I could explain what these reasons were. Elementary steps of this explanation are a clear definition of the questions, a presentation of the scientific basis underlying the answers, and an exposition of the answers themselves. This book is the public account of these steps. It is my hope that having read it people will appreciate why I testified.

IS JOHN DEMJANJUK IVAN?

In many people's perceptions the ethical problem is closely related to the question whether John Demjanjuk is really Ivan or not. If he is not, nobody would argue that exposing the weakness of the identification procedures was wrong. If he is, it could be argued that no good could ever come of such testimony. But we will never know the answer to this question. More important is that the question is irrelevant to an expert witness. The decision to act as a defense witness comes before the trial, at a time that answers to such questions are by definition unknown. The whole purpose of the trial is to enable the court to form an opinion. Expert witnesses can contribute information that helps to form the opinion, but they should not be allowed to thrust their own opinion upon the court. If all parties involved present the best available information, the court's verdict will represent the best approximation of truth. It will always be a subjective judgment, and therefore fallible. But it is not for expert witnesses to criticize the verdict when the verdict seems to be in contradiction with their testimony. The process of translating prior odds into posterior odds is influenced by the experts' likelihoods, but not determined by them. If the reader wants an answer to the question whether John Demjanjuk is Ivan, I can only refer to the court's verdict. It is the best answer we have.

References

Bahrick, H. P., Bahrick, P. O., and Wittlinger, R. P. (1975). Fifty years of memory for names and faces: A cross-sectional approach. *Journal of Experimental Psychology: General, 104*, 54–75.

Bersoff, D. (1979). Comment: The psychologist as expert witness: science in the courtroom? *Maryland Law Review, 38*, 539–620.

Britting v. O.M. (1988). Arrondissementsrechtbank Breda, nr. 7569–86.

Buckhout, R. (1974). Eyewitness Testimony. *Scientific American, 231*, 23–31

Bumber v. O.M. (1985). Arrondissementsrechtbank Amsterdam, nr. 13.007.495.4

Cutler, B. L., Penrod, S. D., and Martens, T. K. (1987). The reliability of eyewitness identification: The role of system and estimator variables. *Law and Human Behavior, 11*, 233–58.

Cutler, B. L., Penrod, S. D., and Stuve, T. E. (1988). Juror decision making in eyewitness identification cases. *Law and Human Behavior, 12*, 41–55.

Darden v. Wainwright (1983). 699 F.2d. 1031, 1043 (11th Cir.).

Darden v. Wainwright (1986). 106 S.Ct. 2464, 2481.

Deffenbacher, K. A. (1980). Eyewitness accuracy and confidence: Can we infer anything about their relationship? *Law and Human Behavior, 4*, 243–60.

Deffenbacher, K. A. (1988). Eyewitness research: The next ten years. In: M. Gruneberg, P. E. Morris, and R. N. Sykes (eds). *Practical Aspects of Memory*, Vol. 1, 20–6, New York: John Wiley & Sons.

De Fouw v. O.M. (1988). Arrondissementsrechtbank Almelo, nr. 88.15802.

Dent, H. R. (1977). Stress as a factor influencing person recognition in identification parades. *Bulletin of British Psychological Society,* **30**, 339–40.

Detterman, D. K. (1981). *Memorandum Re: United States v. Demjanjuk, Case No. C77–923.* Cleveland, manuscript.

Devlin, Rt. Hon. Lord Patrick (chair) (1976). *Report to the Secretary of State for the Home Department of the Departmental Committee on Evidence of Identification in Criminal Cases.* PP.XIX, No. 338. London: HMSO.

Doob, A. N. and Kirshenbaum, H. M. (1973). Bias in police lineups – partial remembering. *Journal of Police Science and Administration* **1**, 287–93.

King, M. (1986). *Psychology In and Out of Court: A Critical Examination of Legal Psychology.* Oxford: Pergamon Press.

Krenten v. O.M. (1986). Arrondissementsrechtbank Rotterdam, nr. 005191–87–VR.

Krijger v. O.M. (1988). Arrondissementsrechtbank Haarlem, nr. 15012362/7–5.

Loftus, E. F. (1974). Reconstructing memory: The incredible eyewitness. *Psychology Today,* **8**, 116–19.

Loftus, E. F. (1979). *Eyewitness Testimony.* Cambridge: Harvard University Press.

Loftus, E. F. (1986). Experimental psychologist as advocate or impartial educator. *Law and Human Behavior,* **10**, 63–78.

Loftus, E. F. (1987). Trials of an expert witness. *Newsweek,* June 29, 10–11.

Loftus, E. F., and Greene, E. (1980). Warning: Even memory for faces may be contagious. *Law and Human Behavior,* **4**, 323–39.

Loftus, E. F., Miller, D. G., and Burns, H. J. (1978). Semantic integration of verbal information into a visual memory. *Journal of Experimental Psychology: Human Learning and Memory,* **4**, 19–31.

Malpass, R. S. (1981). Effective size and defendant bias in eyewitness identification lineups. *Law and Human Behavior,* **5**, 299–309.

Malpass, R. S., and Devine, P. G. (1981). Eyewitness identification: Lineup instructions and the absence of the offender. *Journal of Applied Psychology,* **66**, 482–89.

Malpass, R. S., and Devine, P. G. (1983). Measuring the fairness of eyewitness identification lineups. In: S. M. A. Lloyd-Bostock and B. R. Clifford (eds): *Evaluating Witness Evidence,* 81–102. New York: Wiley and Sons.

Malpass, R. S., and Devine, P. G. (1984). Research on suggestion in lineups and photospreads. In: G. L. Wells and E. F. Loftus (eds). *Eyewitness Testimony: Psychological perspectives*, 64–91. New York: Cambridge University Press.

McCloskey, M. & Egeth, H. E. (1983). Eyewitness identification: What can a psychologist tell a jury? *American Psychologist*, **38**, 550–63.

Neil v. Biggers (1972). 409 US 188; 93 S Ct 575; 34 L Ed 2d 401.

Pfungst, O. (1911). *Clever Hans (the horse of Mr. Van Osten): A contribution to experimental, animal, and human psychology.* (Translated by C. L. Rahn). New York: Holt.

Poelstra v. O.M. (1988). Arrondissementsrechtbank Utrecht, nr. 5682–8.

Rosenthal, R. (1966). *Experimenter effects in behavioral research.* New York: Appleton-Century-Crofts.

Ryan, A. A., Sher, N. M., Moscowitz, N. A., and Einhorn, B. J. (1981). *Government's motion in limine to bar the testimony of defendant's expert psychologist and character witnesses.* Cleveland, Manuscript.

Shapiro, P. N., and Penrod, S. (1986). Meta-analysis of facial identification studies. *Psychological Bulletin*, **100**, 139–56.

United States of America v. Frank Walus (1978). Northern District of Illinois, Eastern Division, no. 77C279.

Vlek, C. A. J., and Wagenaar, W. A. (1979). Judgment and decision under uncertainty. In: J. A. Michon, E. G. J. Eijkman, & L. F. W. de Klerk (eds), *Handbook for Psychonomics*. Amsterdam: North-Holland Publishing Company.

Wagenaar, W. A. (1988a). Calibration and the effects of knowledge and reconstruction in retrieval from memory. *Cognition*, **28**, 277–96.

Wagenaar, W. A. (1988b). The proper seat: A discussion of the position of expert witnesses. *Law and Human Behavior*, **12**, in press.

Wagenaar, W. A., and Boer, J. P. A. (1987). Misleading post-event information: Testing parameterized models of integration in memory. *Acta Psychologica*, **66**, 291–306.

Wagenaar, W. A., and Groeneweg, J. (1988). The memory of concentration camp survivors. *Applied Cognitive Psychology*, in press.

Weinstein, J. B., Mansfield, J. H., Abrams, N., and Berger, M. A. (1983). *Cases and Materials on Evidence* (7th ed.). Mineola, New York: The Foundation Press.

Wijmenga v. O.M. (1988). Arrondissementsrechtbank Amsterdam, nr. 13.024.233.6

The following documents, given in evidence to the Jerusalem Court, were cited in the text:

Tav/46   A copy of the pictures contained in the Trawniki spread.
Tav/57   A copy of the pictures contained in the Album spread.
Tav/58   Identification by Turowski on 10 May 1976.
Tav/60   Identification by Goldfarb on 9 May 1976, 1.00 pm.
Tav/61   Identification by Goldfarb on 9 May 1976, 2.30 pm.
Tav/63   Identification by Rosenberg on 11 May 1976.
Tav/66   Identification by Czarny on 21 September 1976.
Tav/67   Identification by Helman on 29 September 1976.
Tav/69   Identification by Boraks on 30 September 1976.
Tav/70   Identification by Lindwasser on 3 October 1976.
Tav/73   Identification by Turowski on 9 May 1976.
Tav/78   Identification by Epstein on 29 March 1978.
Tav/80   Identification by Epstein on 25 December 1979.
Tav/81   Identification by Rosenberg on 25 December 1979.
Tav/185 Identification by Rajchman on 12 March 1980.
Nun/7   Statement made by Rosenberg in Vienna, 1947.

Index